Vital Energy
Energy for Normal Body Function

Pollution of mind vitiates the vital energies of bodies. A polluted mind always thinks in negative terms and visualizes the dark side of the things to come. Persons with polluted minds commit major crimes.

According to author, spiritualism is the answer to overcome this problem. This will bring peace and happiness, the basic rights of human beings. Spiritualism will help in controlling our unbound desires and save the human beings from dejection. This will also make us realize about the tremendous energy lying within us and its proper utilization.

Vital Energy

Energy for Normal Body Function

B.B. SAHI

New Age Books

ISBN: 978-81-7822-081-9

Revised Edition: Delhi, 2009

First Edition: Delhi, 2002

© Author

Published by
NEW AGE BOOKS
A-44 Naraina Phase-I
New Delhi-110 028 (INDIA)
Email: nab@vsnl.in
Website: www.newagebooksindia.com

Printed in India
at Shri Jainendra Press
A-45 Naraina Phase-I, New Delhi-110 028

This book is dedicated to the readers and their understanding of the self.

This is also dedicated to my strive for spirituality.

Contents

Preface

Modernization has brought about some comforts in life; but unfortunately it has also created lots of problems for the human existence.

The problems can be summed up in one word as *Pollution* including *pollution of the atmosphere, pollution of the roads, pollution of food,* the last but not the least, *pollution of the mind* and character.

People are getting dejected because their *hopes, desires and expectations have become too high, whereas the achievements have gone low; this is because of too many people on the planet earth.* In other words, too many people competing for a single goal.

This pollution has created many physical, mental and psychological ailments, the scientists have therefore diverted their attention towards the ancient scriptures to find a solution to these problems and have started exploring spiritualism once again.

Pollution of mind vitiates the vital energies of bodies, which are directed towards doing wrong things, not liked by the society at large and are considered as criminal acts. A polluted mind always thinks in negative terms and visualizes the dark side of the things to come. Persons with polluted minds commit major crimes which add to the pollution of mind and character and hence a vicious circle. If time and space allows us we shall touch the subjects again in subsequent pages.

21st century will be the century of *spiritualism*. It is thought that spiritualism will spread during the next century to bring *peace* and *happiness* on the earth once again. Keeping this in mind I was inspired to write this book in the common man's language for a common educated person.

Indian philosophy of spiritualism is the oldest philosophy known to human race. The whole world particularly the developed world, is trying to explore and rediscover the basic right of human beings to *peace and happiness*.

Both of these lie within us. If we can control our increasing desires, and look within ourselves to recognize our real identity, we are bound to find peace, which automatically brings a feeling of well-being and happiness.

This book will make you realize the tremendous amount of energy we have within our bodies, which if utilized properly and profitably can bring about the changes needed to make our lives happy and peaceful.

I have tried to combine the modern views with the traditional views of the working of the energy system of the human body. During my research I was very much impressed by the work of Anoda Judith, a somatic therapist, counsellor and teacher of yoga, practising in U.S.A. She has tried to give teaching of Vedas and vital energy system of the human body a modern interpretation.

I have divided this book into smaller chapters keeping in mind that the reader should not get bored. The readers who have even the slightest inclination towards spirituality and self-understanding shall be able to link up the different chapters easily.

B.B. SAHI

Introduction

Our body needs energy for its survival, as well as for performing daily tasks. The heart needs energy to beat and send blood to different parts of the body; The lungs need energy to breath and purify the blood. Energy is *vital* for the existence and sustenance of our body.

There are a number of books available on this subject, which are beyond the understanding of common man. In the modern age, a high percentage of the population of the world is literate and inquisitive to understand the structure and working of our bodies. Since energy is required for performance of any and every task, it is essential to understand the working of the body system.

The aim of this book is to explain in a simple language, how the human body gets its energy, how that energy circulates in the body, how that energy is utilized and distributed, and how we can attain spirituality and increase our horizon of thinking and develop extra sensory perception so that we can understand our body and its working in a better way, what factors influence our particular behavior, and how those can be modified to our advantage. This book shall endeavor to explain in a addition.

According to Vedic teachings the human body is made up of five tattvas or elements *viz. earth, water, fire, air* and *ether.* A definite balance is required between these elements to keep the body in a good functional state. By understanding the energy of the body, we can have a better understanding of the *Self* too, which can help in transformation of our consciousness, which in turn helps in improving our efficiency in day-to-day working, improving our relationships with ourselves and others, and give a better purpose to life. These five elements shall be discussed in detail in a separate chapter.

In the present days and age, everyone is keen to have a complete knowledge of his body and mind, so as to understand its working in a better way. By doing so, one can endeavor to become a perfect individual leading a perfect life.

The vital energy, we are going to discuss in this book is also called *shakti, prana, chi, bio-physical energy, electromagnetic energy, orgone, vital life-force,* or may be known by many different names in different languages. This energy flows through and around the human body as invisible psychic energy, through a network of channels called *Nadis,* which mean *streams.* This energy is distributed by an invisible energy field present around the human physical body called *Aura* (human aura) or *bioplasmic body.* In the bioplasmic body the energy runs in different directions in streams which are thinner than the diameters of a hair, called *Nadis.* These Nadis criss-cross, intermingle, form loops or even become aggregated at places to form circular whirlpool of energy called *chakras.* Here in chakras the energy circulates in clockwise as well as anticlockwise directions like a pendulum of a clock.

These *Chakras* are like manholes of energy, which receive as well as distribute the energy to different parts of the physical body. These 72,000 Nadis are suppose to *pass or criss-cross* the bioplasmic body at the level of umbilicus (belly-button).

According to Itzahak Bentov, "*The human body oscillates up and down due to energy at the rate of seven times per second. This frequency is too high for us to perceive with our limited lumbering sense."*

The Figure of seven is symbolic of seven rainbow colors in Hindu mythology. Maya created world out of seven rainbow hued veils; in Egyptian mythology, it is seven stoles of Isis, in Christianity seven veils of Salome. There are seven phases of solar system. Esoteric constitution of human body has seven planes. Similarly, there are seven main chakras, which energise the human body and mind.

Our ancestors discovered this energy system over ten thousand years ago. The Guru imparted the knowledge of this system by the word of mouth to his disciples. This energy system is described in *Vedas* and *Upanishads* (Hindu scriptures).

A brief description of Vedas and some quotes from Upanishads are given in the next chapters for better understanding of the reader. By the time you finish this book, you will realize the importance of meditation for the modern day and age human being. Therefore, I have made an endeavor to explain the meditation in detail for a beginner, by following which one can make it a part of his daily routine. I am confident readers will definitely find themselves wiser about the understanding of life energy after finishing this book.

1

Elements (Tattvas)

According to Vedic teachings, the human body is composed of five elements, which are:

1. *Earth:* This is the basic element, which forms the solid parts of the body like bones, muscles, hair etc. and nourishes these parts. Its chief character is stability of the body.
2. *Water:* This makes up the body fluids, blood, lymph, saliva etc. and nourishes and replenishes them. 70 per cent of our body is water.
3. *Fire:* This is also called *Ojas.* This is required for digestion (to digest food) and for sexual energy. Vedas worship the *fire,* which means the worship of the *Sun.* The *Sun* represents *fire.* Fire is worshipped because:
    (*a*) it purifies,
    (*b*) it produces light and makes you see clearly,
    (*c*) it amplifies whatever is put into it,
    (*d*) mantras, which are chanted while worshipping the fire, fan different flames, and
    (*e*) fire gives heat and energy.
4. *Air:* Air makes up *Prana* and is required for circulatory system (blood circulation), endocrine glands, nervous system (nerves) and skin. This is required for the

nourishment and viability of the whole body. Air is unstable and expendable. This is *life-force* which fans the FIRE of the body, which is the Energy and sends it to different parts of the body so that they can perform their functions.

5. *Ether:* This is the cosmic element, which provides the space for the growth of the rest of the elements and is represented by the brain, ears and procreating fluids like semen.

Humors

○ These are elements in different forms.
○ Three humors are *Wind, Bile* and *Mucus.*
○ Air element produces *Wind.*
○ Fire element produces *Bile.*
○ Combinations of earth and water produce *Mucus.*

Chakras are playground for the elements. The real players are the elements.

2

Gunas

Gunas are modes of energy, which comprise primordial nature. In unmanifested state, the three gunas are in a state of equilibrium. When this equilibrium is disturbed the manifested state of universe appears.

Hindu mythology believes that the entire cosmos is evolved from *Prakriti* (nature) and Prakriti is made of three gunas or qualities, which correspond with matter, energy and consciousness, which guide our lives.

Nature is Prakriti for the body, whereas body is prakriti for the Soul. Prakriti is self begotten and has three fundamental virtues which are GUNAS.

Prakriti is also synonymous with Female Energy and is contemplated in the following ways:

(*a*) Unmanifest
(*b*) Intellect
(*c*) Super Ego
(*d*) Proper Senses.

Eleven organs of cognition, sense perception and communication have emanated from the Prakriti, these are: Ears, Skin, Eyes, Nose, Tongue, Speech, Hands, Genitalia, Anus, Feet and Mind (in other words, Five Gyan Indries, Five Karam Indries and Mind).

Purusha

Purush or purusha is Self Conscious reality. It is synonymous with Male Energy. According to Vedas, both Purush and Prakriti are Eternal realities, both of them are without an origin, are endless, disembodied, eternal, all pervading and omnipresent. Only Prakriti is non conscious and possesses three fundamental qualities of Rajas, Tamas and Sattva. Prakiriti performs the functions of a seed in phenomenal Evolution and contributes the maternal element in conception, development and birth of Primordial Cosmic Matter (Universe) fecundated by Purush in different stages of Evolution. Purush is indifferent to pleasures and miseries of life.

All of us are born with three gunas. Although character of all these gunas are present in our body/nature, but a particular guna dominates (the other two gunas remain dormant), depending upon the accumulated karmas of our previous births, karmas of our ancestors (pitras) which are embedded in our genes and even the karmas of our community/race (racial characters). Our existence is based on these three gunas called — Sattva, Rajas and Tamas.

1. *Sattva* is satya (truth, essence) god like. It represents mind or consciousness (balancing force) at causal plane. A normal mind in reality is clear and pure, it becomes hazy and polluted by negative thoughts and emotions. A pure mind leads to self-realization. Sattva is a divine nature, which makes the mind explore inwards and tries to unify the heart and the head. It is spiritual quality, which represents intelligence, harmony, peace and love. It makes the soul to transcend (soul's journey upwards) towards realization of the God.

2. *Rajas* is turbulence in mind, which makes the mind to look outwards to seek fulfillment of the desires from the outside world. It is a mind, which is agitated by desires, which includes anger, manipulativeness

and egoistic attitude. Rajas mind seeks *power* and stimulation through entertainment derived by fair or foul means. It represents Energy (kinetic force) at subtle plane. Rajasika qualities are action, turbulence, passion, aggression, competition, pain and strife. Rajasika people become mad for possession of worldly gains. This is a demonic quality and keeps the soul in the middle world, which means attachments, acquisitions and worldly achievements. Rajasika people are usually impatient and inconsistent in dealings.

3. *Tamas* is inertia (dullness, drowsiness, ignorance). Tamas mind is clouded by ignorance and fear creating sloth, sleep, lack of attention and lack of concentration. This mind lacks activity and sensitivity and is dominated by external and subconscious forces leading to animal nature and poor personal hygiene. It represents Matter at physical plane, which is 'Magnetic force'. It is lower quality represented by darkness, obstruction and lethargy. It is animal quality and keeps the soul in the lower worlds. It creates decay and destruction culminating into being harmful to others, leading an aimless life without any goal. The destructive tendencies show soul in a state of descent.

Sattva and Tamas are exactly opposites or two sides of a coin. If *rajas* dominates it gives us energy, if *tamas* dominates it gives us matter as in earth, if *sattva* dominates its gives us spiritual experience as light in the heaven. Whatever we experience in our life is a mixture of matter, energy and intelligence (consciousness).

Rajas and tamas nature go hand in hand, some time one dominates and at other times the other dominates. Rajas creates false imaginations and egoistic ideas.

If Rajas gets in excess it depletes energy through over activity and makes one Tamasika, dull and lethargic. Rajas creates energy, vitality and emotions, whereas Tamas creates energies and allows fixed ideas to take shape.

Sattva is *amrit* (nectar), which is essence of fire element. This nectar is the secretion of the glands in the head that is *Pineal Gland, Hypothalamus* and *Pituitary Gland*, whereas tamas is poison, essence of water element (the metabolic waste of the body). When you remove bad qualities from poison it becomes nectar and if bad qualities are added to nectar it becomes poison.

Rajas is a bridge between sattva and tamas. It can change sattva into tamasa and *vice-versa*, because rajas is energy, which produces illusion (maya). If rajas is controlled anything can be achieved. Only *Shiva* has the power to drink poison and convert it into nectar. Shiva resides in Ajna Chakra (between the two eyebrows), which is higher intelligence. Shiva is your real *Self* or *Soul.* So far you remain in lower chakras, you identify yourself with the senses (illusion), a state of ignorance. But once you reach Shiva, you become Universal-Self. The Shiva can only be realized through meditation (*sadhana*) and to learn this, you need a master to guide you. Hence, tamas (matter) rules lower chakras (Chakras 1, 2 and 3), rajas (energy) rules middle chakras (Chakras 4 and 5) and sattva (consciousness) rules upper chakras (Chakras 6 and 7).

The food we eat influences our gunas and the predominant guna with which we are born influences our food intake.

Sattva or sattvika people eat very little to survive. They prefer nourishing, simple, natural foods, which are low in calories, like fresh milk, fresh vegetables and fruits, natural nuts and wheat.

Rajasika people eat food, which tickles the taste buds, gives lot of energy and heat and is high in calories like meat, milk products, wheat, cooked vegetables etc.

Tamasika people eat anything which comes their way, half-cooked, stale, non-nourishing, leftover foods which are more acid producing and unbalanced.

Sattvika people perform karmas (action), without being attached to its results.

Rajas act with passion, guided by the desire. Tamas act without thinking. Whereas Rishis remain untouched by these three gunas. Discipline, regularity, simplicity, prayer, devotion, self-study, self-analysis, charity, kindness, truthfulness, faith, non-violence, non-stealing, cleanliness and celibacy etc. can enhance Sattvika qualities.

Factors, which influence one's gunas, are:

○ The karmas (the actions) one performs.
○ The time of the day one gets up or sleeps.
○ The acts one performs.
○ The sacrifices one performs.
○ Type of the thoughts one gets.
○ Images one perceives.
○ Karmas of past lives.
○ Mantra one recites.
○ The objects one reveres.
○ Type of people one interacts with.
○ Places habitually visited by an individual.
○ Type of water one drinks/uses.
○ Type of books one studies.
○ Thirst for knowledge of the supreme.

Sattva nature can be improved by Yogic practices, meditation, spiritual cultivation, pro-sattva diet and living life in harmony with one's own constitution. There is a balance between Body, Mind and Nature.

To understand the flow of the energy in the body, let us first understand the constitution of the body.

3

Constitution of Human Body

It was revealed in Upanishads thousands of years ago that human body has a highly developed energy field. Recently, it has been proved scientifically that every *matter* has its electromagnetic energy field.

According to Upanishads the human body is constituted of: *(a)* Energy field (etheric body), *(b)* Self (physical body), and *(c)* Brahma (spirit/soul) — which link the human body with the life in universe.

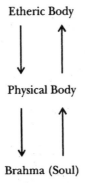

Etheric Body

Physical Body

Brahma (Soul)

An imbalance either between the etheric body and physical body or between physical body and soul will lead to disease.

Theosophy teaches that solar system is seven phase *i.e.*, esoteric constitution of man has seven planes:

1. Physical plane
2. Emotional plane (also called astral body or body of desires.)
3. Mental plane (*i.e.*, plane of perception)
4. Intuitional plane (plane of intuition and imagination)
5. Spiritual plane
6. Monadic plane (or higher plane)
7. Divine plane

Spirit is synonymous with god. Soul is synonymous with higher-self and body is synonymous with lower-self.

Lower-self can be divided into four planes: 1. Etheric Body, 2. Physical Body, 3. Mental Body, and 4. Emotional Body.

1. *Etheric Body:* It is also called bioplasmic body and is the energy house of physical body. This plane energises and vitalises the physical body. This body will be discussed in detail in subsequent pages.

2. *Physical Body:* This is made of organs and systems of solids, liquids and gases and has all the five senses *i.e.*, sight, smell, taste, hearing and tactile sense. In Sanskrit, it is also called the body of *five Indries.*

   In an average individual it is the senses which control the mind but in an evolved individual the mind controls the senses.

3. *Mental Body:* Mental body is 'Chit', or perception driven by the mind. It serves as a vehicle for concrete thinking and helps to develop memory and imagination.

   Most of the things in the world have been created by the power of imagination. The mind creates everything by imagination, which is converted into reality by logic thinking and hard work.

   In mental body it is the 'thought' process which comes into play. THOUGHT is creation of the Mind. An impulse is sent to the brain by either Astral, Mental or Causal body. Brain acts as an Amplifier and amplifies that impulse into a THOUGHT. It is the Thought which creates the faculty of analyzing the situation in a logical way.

4. *Emotional Body:* Emotional Body is also called astral plane or body, and is the seat of desires. All desires *i.e.*, pleasure, pain, fear, courage are all felt in the Emotional body. Emotions play a very important role in our lives. They are the causes of attachments in this world. Most people function at this plane. LOVE represents the highest form of emotions. If Love becomes associated with Attachment it creates pain. Unconditional Love gives pleasure.

4

Vedas and Upanishads

VEDAS

Vedas are the oldest Scriptures of India. Vedas do not belong to any Time or any Religion; it is a misconception to relate them to Hindu religion. Vedas are a Religion in themselves, moreover *Hinduism* is not a Religion, it is a Way of Life. 'Ved' comes from Sanskrit, it is a short form of VID DHATU, where 'Vid' stands for Knowledge (or to Know) and 'Dhatu' stands for matter *i.e.*, self.

SELF is composed of matter which gets destroyed or decayed with Time (Material) but SPIRIT is non-destructible and non-decayable and everlasting. Spirit was there before, it is there now and it will be there in future and this is the basis of the "Theory of Transmigration" of the Spirit/Soul.

Hindus recognize Vedas as the origin of their faith.

There are four Vedas:

1. Rig Veda

This is written in Poetry or Mantras/Hymns which are all in praise of the Creator. It concludes by saying, "Let all the men think alike with One Mind, Let all Hearts unite in Love, Let the goals be common and Let every day be a Valentine day". May every body live a happy and purposeful life?

2. Yajur Veda

Yug means 'Worship'. 'Yajur' comes from Yug. Yug spells out
the rituals for worship.Yug is performed to purify the Prakriti
and soul, using hymns from Rig Veda.

3. Sam Veda

'Sam' means Shanti and Shanti is derived from Shant. Here
the Mind is set to path of peace by singing Rig Veda hymns
on seven fundamental notes of Indian music i.e., Sa, Re, Ga,
Ma, Pa, Da, Ne. Sam Veda has a detailed description of these
notes. It is said that these notes be sung by a trained priest to
ensure the grace of the Supreme creator.

4. Atharv Veda

'Atharv' means Prohit.Prohit is a learned person who has
perfected the knowledge of 'Brahma', the Creator. Atharv
Veda acts as a 'Prohit', which has Mantras in the form of
Hymns as well as prose to ward off evils as well as hardships
and destroy enemies. It also contains Hymns related with
creation and its wonders. Ayurveda is also a part of Atharv
Veda.

All the Vedas teach us the ways of perfection, attainment
of Bliss and realization of the Truth by following any path
with faith and loyalty purusing the diverse routes. That is how
Vedas have no connection with any Religion. Any way when
Vedas were written there were no religions in existence.

'Purana' is a path to achieve Pursharath (Action). Hence
Creation and dissolution of Universe, Dynasties of Solar and
Lunar races, Different cycles of Time and Biographies of
different good and bad Monarchs are the Topics dealt with
in 'Puranas'. There are 18 Puranas.

Vedic teachings mean, not only teaching of Vedas but also
of Upanishads, Sutras, Brahmanas and Aranyakas. All these
texts are considered to be originally revealed knowledge
called in Sanskrit as 'Shruti.'

*SHRUTI is synonymous with Vedas, it is not what is heard and
it is what is supposed to be heard. Vedas were created with intuitive*

knowledge of the sages, who did not compose them, but saw them and what they saw is 'Shruti'. When they memorized what they saw, they communicated the knowledge to their brains and that is 'Samriti' which was finally written down and decoded by other sages/rishis.

'Smriti' was evolved from Vedas. From Samriti 'Puranas' were derived and from Puranas came the History.

Vedic literature includes the above mentioned texts as well as Puranas, Mahabharata, Bhagavad Gita and Ramayana which are the 'Epics'.

Rishi Vyas, compiled most of the Vedic literature except Ramayana, which was compiled by 'Rishi Balmiki'.

'Puranas' have been described as the fifth Veda in literature.

UPANISHADS

The highest aspect of religious truth is called the *Upanishads*. Upanishad means sitting near a guru *devotedly*.

Adisankara defines it as the knowledge of *Brahma/Soul*.

The Knowledge, that destroys the bonds of ignorance and leads to supreme goal of freedom, which ultimately leads to *emancipation*.

Up to today 108 Upanishads have been found.

'Adisankara' recognized 16 out of 108 as authentic.

Out of these 10 are thought to be principal, out of which I am going to quote some in the next chapter.

Quotes from Upanishads

1. Kath Upanishad

"*Brahma* is Self, is deeply hidden in all, but is not revealed to all. Through self, man experiences sleeping and wakening states. The soul, which enjoys fruits of action, is the self ever present within us, as the lord of time past, present and future. It is immortal self, which is called 'BRAHMA.'

Brahma, the absolute impersonal existence when associated with power, is called *'Maya.'*

"Above the *mind* is the *intellect*, above intellect is *Ego* above *Ego* is the *unmanifest,* the primal cause above which is *Brahma.*"

"*Brahma* is the all-prevailing spirit, the unconditioned, whom nobody can behold with eyes, because it is *formless.* Yet, it revels in the *heart* through *self-control* and *meditation.*"

"When all senses are still, the *mind* at rest and *Intellect* is steady, that is the "*highest blissful state.*"

"Calmness of senses and mind is *Yoga,* and the person who attains Yoga is freed from *delusion.*"

2. Mundaka Upanishad

"Those who know *Brahma* say that there are two kinds of knowledge: the *higher knowledge* by which one knows changeless reality *i.e., Brahma* and the *lower knowledge* is the knowledge of Vedas (four Vedas: *Rig, Sama, Yajur, Atharv*) which describe the ceremonies, grammar, etymology, astronomy and phonetics."

"As a plant grows from a seed, similarly does the Universe from eternal *Brahma* with the Union of *Prakriti (Nature).*"

"The wise, self controlled and tranquil souls who practise *austerity* and *meditation* are freed from all impurities and attain *Brahma.*"

"He is active knowledge, supreme goodness, hidden in the *heart, self-luminous, refuge* of all and the *supreme goal.*"

"When the mind is illuminated by the power of meditation, the divine, the blissful and the immortal know the supreme."

"He, who has realized self, is satisfied of all hunger. He who longs for *HIM,* will find himself revealed in his true being. The weak, the thoughtless or those who do not meditate cannot realize the self. Once you have *realized self* you are filled with *joy* and become *tranquil* in mind and free from *passion.*"

"When the death overtakes this body, the vital energy enters the cosmic force, the senses dissolve in their cause, and the *Karma* and *Soul* enter *Brahma.* He, who knows his

Brahma, is *Brahma,* is beyond sorrows and evil and becomes *immortal.*"

3. Taitatthirya Upanishad

"He who knows *Brahma* attains everything. *Brahma* is only *reality, pure knowledge, infinity* which develops in your heart."

"Out of *Brahma* who is self, comes *Ether.* From *Ether* comes *Air.*

From *air* comes *fire,* from *fire* comes *water,* from *water* comes *earth.*

From *earth* comes *vegetation. Vegetation* produces *food.*

Food makes and nourishes *body,* which is the physical sheath of the self. Inside physical sheath is the *vital* sheath, which has the same form.

Through the vital sheath the senses perform their functions and this sheath decides the *length of life.*"

"He, who worships the *vital* sheath as *Brahma,* lives a *complete* and *full life span.*"

"Encased in the *vital* sheath, is *mental* sheath, which also has the same form. Inside the *mental* sheath is the *intellectual* sheath. Encased in the *intellectual* sheath is *Ego* sheath."

"And encased in the Ego sheath is *Brahma.* Before creation *Brahma* existed as *unmanifest* and from this *unmanifest* was created the *manifest,* so from *himself he created himself.* Hence he is *self-existent.*"

4. Chhandogya Upanishad

"A man, who worships *self,* is free from *grief, hunger, thirst* and *disease.* There is only *self* to be *sought after* and *realized.* He, who *learns* about the *self, obtains the world* and *desires.*"

"The essence of all beings is earth, the essence of earth is water, the essence of water is plants, the essence of plants is man, the essence of man is speech, the essence of speech is holy knowledge (Veda), the essence of Veda is Sama Veda (word, tone, sound), the essence of Sama Veda is OM."

5. *Brhadaranyaka Upanishad*

Since everything is pervaded by *death* and is subject to death, one can *overcome* death by becoming *one with self i.e., Brahma. Brahma* is the *liberator* who helps to overcome *death*.

The *self* is that which cannot see but is the *seer of the sight*, which cannot hear but is *the hearer of the sound*, the *thinker of the thoughts, knower of the knowledge i.e., self,* which is within all.

Everything that is not self, perishes.

The *self* is beyond *hunger, thirst, grief, delusion, fear* and *death.*

Once you have *realized* the *self* there is *no* craving for *progeny, wealth* or *Moksha i.e., Salvation.*

"Whosoever worships another divinity than his self, thinking, 'He is one, I am another', knows not — One should worship with the thought that He is one self, for therein all these become one. This self is the foot print of that all — just as verily, by following a foot print one may find cattle that have been lost — he who reveres the self alone as dear — what he hold dear, verily, will not perish."

Rishi Vyasa compiled most of the Vedic literature except Ramayana, which was compiled by Tulsidas. 'Puranas' have been described as fifth Veda in literature.

Upanishads

○ The highest aspect of religious truth is called the *Upanishads*.

○ Upanishad means sitting near a Guru *devotedly.*

○ Adi Shankara defines it as the *knowledge of Brahma/ Soul.*

○ The knowledge that destroys the bonds of ignorance and leads to supreme goal of freedom, which ultimately leads to *emancipation*.

○ Up to today 108 Upanishads have been found.

○ Adi Shankara recognized '16 out of 108 as authentic'.

Out of these, ten are thought to be principal. I am going to quote some of these in the next chapter.

5

Human Aura
(Bio-plasmic or Etheric Body)

The vital force, which energizes the human body, comes from the *bio-plasmic body* also called *etheric body, energy body* or *human aura.* This energy body looks after requirements of energy in the physical body under different circumstances.

There is a detailed description of human body energy system in *Upanishads,* which are Hindu scriptures and date back to over 3000 BC.

Old Chinese Testaments also describe the body energy system which they divided into meridians and based their system of medicine of Acupuncture/Acupressure on these meridians. "You are looking charming", or "you are glowing with success", these remarks you hear so many times from people. These refer to Human Aura.

WHAT IS AN AURA?

Aura or human energy field is a complete shadow of human body which surrounds the body. It has been named as *Sthool Sharir* in Upanishads. This is the energy body which surrounds all parts and organs of physical body. This is also called *Etheric Body* which can not be visualized by untrained human eye. It is very clear that our ancestors had extraordinary developed sensory/Extra sensory perceptions and Intuitive system that they could visualize the Energy body/system, which we can not preceive. Probably our ancestors lived in a much higher dimension as compared to us or were vibrating at a different frequency than our bodies.

Western researchers were not aware of this system till recently, when they started exploring it.

○ *Aura* is personal energy field, which consists of *electromagnetic* particles radiating from the body in several layers including sound waves, which try to build up a harmonious relationship with the Gravity.

○ The *Aura* is a *Greek* word meaning *breeze* or *air*. This air or energy emanates from your body.

○ Not only every living thing has an *Aura*, but this invisible energy also permeates *inanimate objects* like mountains, rocks etc., which release energy in the *cosmos.*

○ Even the *sun, earth, moon* and other planets have their own *auras*. Rings of *Saturn* or gaseous clouds of energy around *Jupiter are also electro-magnatic emissions from these planets.*

○ *Aura* is often depicted as a *halo.*

○ Your Aura is your reflection.

○ Those people, who can visualize *auras*, describe them as rainbow of colors radiating out of the body.

○ The *human aura* is said to have seven pure colors. The first layer closest to the body relates to *health*, the outer most layer, is *spiritual* layer or the layer depicting how you want to be perceived by others.

○ *Aura* or Auric field reveals your *personality, moods, emotions, actions,* and how your life is changing with circumstances.

○ You can learn to sense your own *aura* or *aura* of others to find your compatibility with others.

○ You must have heard people saying that a particular place or a particular person emits positive rays of energy. You feel like being in his/her company. People, who emit negative rays, are repulsive to you. One can find compatibility between the two *auras* by attraction or repulsion. Aura of one person may attract or repel aura of another person depending upon the compatibility of auras. Compatibility of auras helps in developing and maintaining relationships with other individuals.

○ 'Vastu Shastra' determines the compatibility of human aura with a place, a piece of land, a dwelling place or a work place.

○ By adapting your immediate environment, you can allow positive or beneficial energy to enter your body.

○ If you can understand the energy you radiate from your body, you can learn to bring *harmony* to your self or with others.

○ You should learn to understand or love your *aura*.

○ You may energize your aura by meditation or holding a quartz crystal firmly in your hand and concentrating on the crystal, you will find your own *auric energy* merging with *crystal energy*. Crystals emit very strong energy.

History of Aura

○ Existence of *aura* was described by Indian and Chinese Mystics as long as 4000 BC. *Acupuncture* or *Acupressure* (Chinese way of healing) believes that energy runs in *meridians*. By applying needles and pressure, flow of energy can be increased or decreased in a meridian or a particular part of the body.

○ 500 BC in *Persia*, a form of color therapy was used for healing, based on the light that radiated from an individual.

○ Throughout the ages many people have claimed seeing *auras* particularly around *saints, religious* or *spiritual figures*.

○ With the development of the aura-*imaging* camera towards the end of 20th century, there is now tangible physical proof of the existence of *auras*.

○ *Paracelsus*, a scientist in Switzerland in 16th century, described a vital force emanated from human body. He also believed that quality of light which emanated was the key to a person's state of health. The colors of light were divided into two groups, those with *black* hue represented illness and imbalance of energy, whereas those with *white* hue represented well being and harmony.

○ In early 1800 an *Austrian* physician, *Franz Anton Mesmer* proposed that universe was filled with *ether*, which carried vibrations, which has a direct effect on other living bodies. He also confirmed *healing power of magnets*, and his own hands transmitted energy and he termed it as *animal magnetism*.

○ *Dr. Walter Kilner*, in 1869, in London was fascinated by clairvoyant's claims of seeing *human aura* (clairvoyant people have extra sensory perceptions and can visualize those things, which ordinary people cannot). He called it. He researched human electrical field, using dyes, glass lenses, and screen and concluded that Aura can be seen.

○ In 1939 a *Soviet* scientist, *Semyon Kirlian*, came with a way of photographing the *aura* using electrical plates. This is still being used today.

○ In 1980 *Guy Coggins*, an *American* inventor, developed an *aura imaging technique*. He used a special camera to produce full spectrum of colors of *aura*. According to Coggins, the camera receives the light waves electronically and converts the energy impulses into *auric image* with the help of a computer.

In 1998, Harry Oldfield, a biologist and scientist from London, developed a P.I.P. (*Polycontrast Interference*

Photography) system, which is computer software when connected to a video camera and computer; you can scan and visualize the whole body energy system including Chakras, which project on to a screen.

Harry Oldfield suggests that human energy field is like a template or network of energy points with which the physical molecules of body are aligned.

Now cameras are available to photograph the Aura, what lacks is the trained eye to interpret it.

Aura can be felt, seen, heard, smelt and touched.

Colors of the Aura

The colors of your aura are vibrations of energy, which swirling lights of particles that are given off from the electro-magnetic charge of your energy field. The vibrations form waves, which together make up the electro-magnetic spectrum. These include infrared waves, visible light, x-rays, ultraviolet radiation, gamma rays and radio waves.

The distance between the crests of the waves is *wavelength* and number of waves per second is the *frequency*. Longer the wavelength lower the frequency.

The human eye can see pure colors — red, orange, yellow, green, blue, indigo, violet, from lowest to highest vibrations.

Each color in the *aura* corresponds to certain quality that reflects your personality, mood, and feelings.

People with trained eye and strong *intuitive* skills can see the *changing colors of the aura.*

Interpretations of some of the *aural colors* are:

○ Violet ——*Signifies*——➤ Spiritual Growth, Imagination

○ Blue ——*Signifies*——➤ Intuition, Sensitivity

○ Green ——*Signifies*——➤ Growth, Balance of Mind, Ambitions

○ Yellow ——*Signifies*——➤ Excitement, Optimism, Mental Clarity

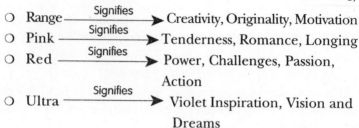

- ○ Range ——— *Signifies* ——→ Creativity, Originality, Motivation
- ○ Pink ——— *Signifies* ——→ Tenderness, Romance, Longing
- ○ Red ——— *Signifies* ——→ Power, Challenges, Passion, Action
- ○ Ultra ——— *Signifies* ——→ Violet Inspiration, Vision and Dreams

People who have *ultraviolet colored aura* are *creative, inventive,* and *eccentric.* They have powerful *psychic abilities* and *amazing insight.*

The *aura* colors seen via the aura imaging camera depend on the subject's mood, personality, and balance between mind, body and spirit, at the time of photographing.

One can study one's character, mind, emotional status and physical health by the study of one's own *Aura.*

The Aura is also called Etheric Body or Bio-plasmic body.

The Aura can be divided into *(a)* Inner Aura *(b)* Outer Aura *(c)* Health rays or health Zone of Aura.

Etheric is a state between energy and matter. Lately it has been proved that even matter has got energy.

Structure of Aura

Inner Aura

The Inner Aura takes exactly the shape of the physical body and is full of energy. The inner aura is situated about 10 to 15 centimetres away from the body. Every part or organ of the physical body has its own aura *i.e.,* head has its own aura and so has the index finger. Heart has its own aura and so has the liver. There may be bulge or retraction in the aura at localized places, showing congestion or depletion of energy at those places. Energized hands can feel the inner aura and when the hands reach near the aura it feels a push or resistance (see picture on page 29).

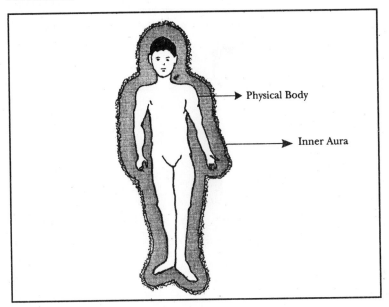

Picture of a figure depicting different parts of aura.

Health Ducts (Health Aura)

From the surface of the physical body arise bio-plasmic ducts projecting perpendicularly interpenetrating with the inner aura and extending up to the outer aura. These bio-plasmic ducts project at 90 degree from the physical body surface, and open on the outer aura as bio-plasmic holes.

These ducts act as channels, which help in expulsion (throwing out) of toxins, waste products and germs from the body.

If the physical body is diseased, health ducts drop and droop or get entangled and can not perform their functions properly, making the physical body susceptible to infections, because capacity of health ducts to expel toxins and bacteria is hampered (see picture on page 30).

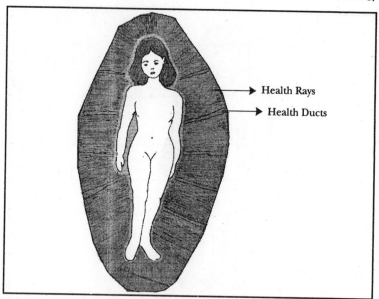

Health Rays

Health Ducts

Picture of figure depicting health ducts.

Outer Aura

Beyond the health ducts there is another energy field
called the Outer Aura, which interpenetrates the health
ducts and Inner Aura. It extends normally up to about 75
centimetres from the physical body.

This is usually oval in shape pointing downwards and its
color depends upon the physical, emotional and mental
status of the body. During sickness holes appear in the Outer
Aura through which energy flows out, hence Outer Aura acts
as a protective shield for the body energy. The Etheric and
Physical bodies are intimately connected to each other.

It is said that a disease manifests itself first in the Etheric
body and affects the physical body after a latent period.

Since the etheric body is controlled by mind to a larger
extent the mind also affects the physical body (see picture on
page 31).

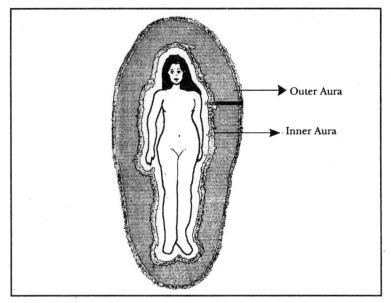

Picture of figure of outer aura.

In a healthy body, the energy field is ample, complex, coherent and dynamic. When we are happy and relaxed the aura is bigger and fluffier, whereas in illness and during mental tension the field or aura contracts and shows cracks. This makes it essential that we take good care of our bodies. A healthy body is capable of developing lots of psychic abilities like *intuition, reasoning, power* etc.

Body workers, energy healers, yoga practitioners and meditators usually have a highly charged energy field (aura). Energy always flows through *thought* and *imagination*.

The Aura is surrounded by subtler energies called subtle bodies or subtle atmosphere which is thought to represent an aspect of our physical, mental, emotional and spiritual experiences. These bodies represent a single energy field which radiates out from each of us to affinity, which means our body energy is inter-penetrating/overlapping with energies of every body else in this universe, which proves that we are all part of one Supreme (Mother) energy called 'Universal Cosmic Energy'.

Etheric Body (Bio-plasmic Body)

Energy is synonymous with *Prana, Chetna, Chi, Shakti* and many other names in different languages.

Functions of Etheric (bio-plasmic) body are:

1. It absorbs vital energy from Cosmos, Sun and Earth, modifies it and distributes it to different parts of body for proper functioning. Without Prana a person *dies.*
2. It acts as a module for physical body to maintain its shape, form and characteristics. If Etheric body is defective the physical body will follow suit.
3. Etheric body through *Chakras* controls the functions of nervous system and endocrine system of the physical body.
4. Etheric body through its protective shield protects physical body from entry of bacteria hence prevents the infections.
5. Etheric body is the vehicle for energy.
6. Etheric body is a whole unified organism, which has its own electro-magnetic field.
7. Emotions affect etheric body.
8. Stimulation of certain points in the etheric body can activate certain psychic abilities. In psychic healing there is flow of energy from healer to healee.

Structure of the Etheric Body

The Etheric body is made up of channels through which energy flows, these channels can be compared to the nerves in the physical body, these are called *Nadis* or streams.

Maximum concentration of energy is along the spinal column because most of the spinal nerves come out from here and supply energy to different parts of the body. Hence most of the functions of the body are controlled by the spinal nerves.

NADI

Nadis are channels or streams very fine in diameter (less than the diameter of a hair) through which energy is directed to different parts of the body. These Nadis have been classified as large, medium and small depending upon their length and diameter. These Nadis also take energy to and from the energy main holes called *Chakras*.

There are 72000–125000 Nadis which aggregate at or around Manipur Chakra, the seat of Fire.

There are nine doors through which energy or prana enter the body, these are two eyes, two nostrils, two ears, mouth, anus and genitalia.

Energy moving with breath fans the body fire and mind, is carried to these doors, so that it can enjoy that energy by experiencing the outside world.

These Nadis of energy enable us to control our ego, mind and senses.

Three most important Nadis are:

1. Susumana Nadi

This is also called fire channel, the central channel that runs in the center of the spinal column associated with the spinal cord. It starts from Muladhara Chakra and ascends to Sahasarara (Crown) Chakra. This is supposed to be the main Nadi supplying energy to all the Chakras and from one Chakra to another. Susumana Nadi also represents *Shiva* in Hindu mythology and it is supposed to be fiery red in color.

Susumana pierces all the chakras; it's like a chain of lights, extremely subtle, awakener of pure knowledge, whose true nature is pure consciousness. She shines because of the presence of the 'Kundalini'. Because 'Kundalini' traverses this Nadi to unite with SHIVA, hence this is the source of all bliss.

This Nadi represents the holy and divine path and facilitates the process of meditation, spirituality and academic pursuits.

2. Ida Nadi

This is also called Chandar (Moon) Nadi and carries cool energy. It also starts from Muladhara Chakra and ascends along the left side of the spinal column criss crossing each Chakra and finally passes through the left nostril to reach Ajna Chakra where it unites with Pingla Nadi. Ida Nadi is also compared to *Yamuna River* because the flow of this river is very quiet and calm. This is said to be pale in color.

In Vastu Shastra, it is thought that Ida Nadi controls Eastern and Northern directions. Creative work, culture, research and art are all attributed to the Northern Current flow. Maintaining the Ida Flow gives worldly goods and divine pleasures.

3. Pingla Nadi

This is also called Surya (Sun) Nadi, which carries hot energy. It also starts from Muladhara Chakra and ascends along the right side of the spinal column criss crossing the different Chakras; it passes through right nostril to end at Ajna Chakra by joining Ida Nadi. This Nadi is compared with *River Ganga*, the course of which is very rough and noisy. It is red in color.

If your right nostril works more efficiently, it increases your appetite and other enjoyments, whereas if left nostril works more efficiently then the appetite and other enjoyments are decreased.

Vastu Shastra says that Pingla Nadi controls the Western and Southern directions. All violent and destructive forces, weapons, torture are attributed to the Southern flow. Blocking Pingla Flow avoids destruction and violent tendencies.

It is the Susumana Nadi through which Kundalini Shakti rises. It is essential for Ida and Pingla Nadis to work in harmony to force Kundalini upwards.

Right nostril pushing more hot energy through Pingla Nadi, increases the pulse rate and blood pressure whereas left nostril pushes more cool energies through Ida Nadi, which decreases the blood pressure and calms the nerves. These Nadis often meet and are connected with one another at ethereal plexuses called *Chakras* and these Chakras can only be perceived by an enlightened mind.

Susumana, Ida and Pingla Nadis all start from Muladhara Chakra and ascend to Ajna Chakra, with Susumana in the center, Ida on the left and Pingla on the right side of the spinal cord. From Ajna Chakra, Ida gets connected with the left nostril whereas Pingla gets connected with the right nostril, while the Susumana rises to Sahasrara (Crown) Chakra.

Two basic paths to reach Shiva or Susumana Nadi are 'path of knowledge' and 'path of devotion' (Bhakti). Path of knowledge is through Pingla (Sun) Nadi that is why all ancient Rishis used to worship Sun and meditate on Sun. When you look at Sun, you virtually become blind to every thing else and you realize only one reality. So the Sun worshipper follows Ganga River.

Those who follow the path of devotion go via Ida Nadi or follow Yamuna River, which is longer than Ganga; hence its follower takes longer time to realize the supreme.

All these three Nadis *i.e.*, Susumana, Ida and Pingla are classified as large Nadis.

Amongst the medium sized Nadis are mentioned the names of *Kuhu, Saraswati, Gandhari, Varuni* and *Pusha* Nadis.

Small Nadis have not been given any particular names.

6

Chakras

Chakras mean *wheel*, which act as storehouses of energy. They are situated in the bio-plasmic or energy body and function as centers for receiving and assimilating the *life-force* or Vital Energy. These are also called 'Astral Centers'. The energy circulates in a chakra in clockwise as well as anti-clockwise directions like a pendulum.

The chakra system originated in India more than ten thousand years ago. These have been mentioned in Vedas and Upanishads. Maharishi Patanjali was the person who laid the foundation of Yoga.

Yoga means to yoke (connect), a discipline designed to yoke together the individual with the divine, or the human vital energy with the universal cosmic energy. It may also be interpreted as union of the lower brain with the upper brain or union of the right hemisphere of the brain with the left hemisphere of the brain. Lower brain or lower-Self is represented by spinal cord, medulla and mid-brain. Upper brain or upper-Self is represented through two hemispheres of cerebrum right and left, cerebellum, thalamus and hypothalamus. Right hemisphere of the cerebrum represents Shakti (crude female energy), which involves pattern recognition, intuition, sensitivity and creative insight. Left cerebral hemisphere represents Shiva (refined male energy), which is responsible for rationalism, analytical sense and critical thinking. Hence, right side of the body is male (Shiva) and left side of the body is female *i.e.*, shakti (Because the left cerebral hemisphere controls right side of the body and the right cerebral hemisphere controls left side of the body).

All that manifests is *power*. What is manifest? Mind, Life and Matter. Hence, mind, life and matter are *power* and power is Shakti. If there is power there must be a power holder, which in Sanskrit is called Shaktimaan. And here the Shaktimaan is *Shiva* and *Shakti* is universal mother.

There is no Shakti without Shakti holder and there is no Shakti holder if there is no Shakti. Hence, they are meant for each other.

Siva is consciousness (Chit).

Shakti is Bliss (Anand).

Mind is consciousness and matter is Bliss.

Consciousness is static (Sthir) and Shakti (Bliss) is moving.

Human beings are static power holders (Siva, Shakti-maan), which is pure consciousness (Chit). Hence, Mind and body are manifestations of Shiva and Shakti (Shiva-Shakti).

This proves that Human Being (Man) is expression of *power*.

Yoga teaches to raise this power to its perfect expression (unlimited experience) because unlimited experience is whole (Purna) or 'perfect Bliss', whereas worldly experience is limited.

All the physiological and psychological changes arise because of mutations of gunas and elements. In everyday Yoga we try to connect our physical body with the cosmic energy by the help of certain exercises called *Asanas* and by certain breathing exercises called *Pranayam*, whereas the mental connection can be established through a process called *Meditation*.

Human body is composed of opposites like good and bad,

protons and neutrons, acid and alkali and these opposites make humans experience *duality and bipolarity.*

Chakras interchange the energy with the nerve ganglions situated along the spine of the physical body and influence the endocrine glands of the body to produce the exact amount of secretions required for a particular action.

These chakras have no physical entity in themselves, yet they have a strong effect on the working of human (physical) body, because these chakras are programmed deeply into our mind-body interface. They control all our emotions and different organs including endocrine glands of the physical body, and regulate their secretions.

These chakras are roughly 5 cm in diameter and have a definite location in relation to the body and amongst themselves. There are seven major chakras, six of them are situated along the spinal column of the physical body whereas the seventh chakra, which is not a chakra in true sense is situated on the top of the head.

They take the shape of a Lotus, the petals of which can open in either direction. If properly opened or developed they bring more energy from the higher planes.

Kundalini Shakti described in a subsequent chapter is a manifestation of power in Etheric matter on the physical plane. Chakras, when fully aroused by the 'Serpent Fire' (Kundalini), bring down in physical consciousness the quality inherent in the corresponding Astral Center. Hence, the Chakras become the windows of connections between the Physical and Astral Body. The body of senses *i.e.*, physical body now can share all the advantages brought by awakening of the Etheric Centers or Chakras and this change takes place by the force of Kundalini Shakti, which exists in the Etheric matter at the physical plane. This in turn triggers the higher centers, which bring the Astral energy to the physical consciousness, when this happens a person starts living at Astral plane.

Kundalini Shakti has seven coverings and one of these

coverings is shed at each Chakra, when Kundalini Shakti starts rising.

These seven chakras are:

1. Muladhara Chakra (base chakra) or first chakra
2. Svadhishthana Chakra (sex chakra) or second chakra
3. Manipura Chakra (naval chakra) or third chakra
4. Anahata Chakra (heart chakra) or fourth chakra
5. Vishuddha Chakra (sound chakra) or fifth chakra
6. Ajna/Agya Chakra (third eye) or sixth chakra
7. Sahasrara Chakra (crown chakra) or seventh chakra

Some learned rishis thought that there are nine chakras. As mentioned earlier, Sahasrara Chakra is not considered as a true chakra. Hence, they described six chakras in the bio-plasmic body and three chakras inside the head at the Astral level, these chakras were named as *Golata*, *Lalata* and *Lalana*. These three chakras are thought to be beyond physical and spiritual levels, perhaps these are at *Astral level*.

These energy chakras have been compared to petals of lotus, because lotus is a symbol of purity. It lives in the mud but rises above it. Mud is compared to Maya (illusion). Lotus opens at sunrise and closes at sunset. The lotuses of six chakras open only when Kundalini shakti is present in them, otherwise these lotuses remain closed. Each Chakra has 4, 6, 10, 12, 16, and 2 petals in ascending order and each petal represents *Bija Mantra* for that chakra, by reciting (*japa*) of this *mantra* one can strengthen a particular chakra. Sahasrara (*crown*) chakra is said to be 1000 petals lotus because it connects with the mother energy called the universal cosmic energy.

Chakras only function when Kundalini shakti moves in them, at all other times the function of chakra is superficial related to function of endocrine glands and other body organs including nerve ganglia and circulatory system.

Chakras are knots, which bind ego (ahamkara) with self-identification and plug ego into the elements. It is always good to allow the chakras to open on their own, when they are ready, which happens when three coverings of gunas have been removed from the kundalini by meditation.

The six chakras have been identified with the nerve plexuses of the physical body:

Name of the Chakra	Name of the Nerve Plexus	Place in the Physical Body
Muladhara Chakra	Sacro coccygeal nerve plexus	Near the tail of the backbone
Svadhishthana Chakra	Lumbosacral nerve plexus	At the back of genitalia (four fingers above the tail of the backbone)
Manipura Chakra	Solar plexus	Opposite the belly-button or navel
Anahata Chakra	Cardiac plexus	Middle of the chest
Vishuddha Chakra	Laryngeal plexus	In the neck
Ajna Chakra	Cerebellum and its lobes	On the forehead between two eyebrows called 'Gleabella'

Sahasrara Chakra (Crown Chakra)

Sahasrara Chakra (crown chakra) is located at the top of the head above the portion of the brain connecting the right and left brain. It is situated over the vertex.

The endocrine glands of the physical body are the counter-part of the chakras in the etheric body and are energized by these chakras. Chakras, which relate with different endocrine glands, are given on page 42.

Chakra		Endocrine Glands
Muladhara	(first)	Adrenal glands, situated above the kidneys
Svadhishthan	(second)	Gonads (testes and ovaries)
Manipura	(third)	Pancreas, liver and adrenal glands
Anahata	(fourth)	Thymus
Vishuddha	(fifth)	Thyroid and para thyroid glands.
Ajna	(sixth)	Pitutary glands, hypothalamus.
Sahasrara	(seventh)	Pineal gland, thalamus, hypothalamus

Each chakra represents an element, which is described in the following table:

Chakra	Element
First Chakra	Earth
Second Chakra	Water
Third Chakra	Fire
Fourth Chakra	Air
Fifth Chakra	Sound
Sixth Chakra	Light
Seventh Chakra	Thought

These chakras also influence and control functions and working of certain organs in the physical body which are enumerated below:

Chakra	Organs Influenced
Muladhara Chakra	Stomach and rectum.
Svadhishthana Chakra	Kidneys, bladder, reproductive organs and large intestines.
Manipura Chakra	Pancreas, stomach, spleen, gall bladder, small intestines and sympathetic nervous system.
Anahata Chakra	Heart, lungs, vagus nerves and blood circulation.
Vishuddha Chakra	Vagus nerves, respiratory system, esophagus (food pipe).
Ajna Chakra	Lower brain, left eye and nose.
Sahasrara Chakra	Higher brain and right eye.

Chakras also relate themselves with different *senses* of the body, which are:

Chakra	Senses
Muladhara Chakra	Smell
Svadhishthana Chakra	Taste
Manipura Chakra	Sight
Anahata Chakra	Touch
Vishuddha Chakra	Speech and hearing
Ajna Chakra	Sixth sense

Different chakras are represented by different sounds, if a person wishes to energize those particular chakras, they can meditate on those particular sounds by chanting specific mantras, which are given in the chart below:

Chakra	Mantra	Sound
Muladhara (Base) Chakra	Lam	Ohh
Svadhishthana (Sex) Chakra	Vam	Oooo
Manipura (Navel) Chakra	Ram	Ahh
Anahata (Heart) Chakra	Yam	Ayy
Vishuddha (Sound) Chakra	Ham	Eeee
Ajna (Third eye) Chakra	OM	Mmm
Sahasrara (Crown) Chakra	–	Nugg

These chakras are also influenced by certain planets and signs, which are given on page 44.

Lower chakras are closer to the earth, hence are related to practical matters of life like survival, movements *i.e.*, locomotion, action and sexuality etc. whereas the upper chakras are associated with love, communication, intuition and spirituality.

Minor Chakras and Mini-Chakras

There are 21 minor Chakras and 49 mini-Chakras. All minor chakras develop during the last three months of fatal life and are situated on the surface of the physical body on the following places:

Chakra	Planets	Signs
Muladhara	Saturn & Mars	Aries, Taurus, Scorpio & Capricorn
Svadhishthana	Venus, Mercury, Moon & Mars	Cancer, Libra & Scorpio
Manipura	Sun, Jupiter, Mercury & Mars	Leo, Virgo & Sagittarius
Anahata	Sun, Venus & Saturn	Leo & Libra
Vishuddha	Mars, Venus & Uranus	Gemini, Taurus & Aquarius
Ajana	Mercury, Venus & Uranus	Sagittarius, Aquarius & Pisces
Sahasrara	Saturn & Neptune	Capricorn & Pisces

1. One behind each eye
2. One in each supra clavicular region
3. One over each breast
4. One in epigestrium
5. Two over spleen
6. One over liver
7. One over thymus
8. One over each palm
9. One in each groin
10. One on each iliacfossa for gonads
11. One behind each knee
12. One over each sole

The whole bio-plasmic body is studded with energy channels called nadis, which have already been described in the chapter on Human Aura.

Before we embark upon functions of various main chakras in detail I would like to mention a different classification of main chakras.

Some people who are supposed to have better knowledge of chakras consider a slightly different classification of major Chakras. They think that there are two Manipura Chakras one in front and one at the back. Similarly, there are two Anahata chakras, one at the front and one at the back. There is a chakra at the back opposite the umbilicus (belly-button) called 'Meng-mein Chakra' and there is a Navel chakra in front of the umbilicus. There is also a Forehead chakra just above Ajna chakra. These chakras influence or control the following organs:

1. *Meng-mein Chakra* controls adrenal glands and kidneys, which help in maintaining the blood pressure.

   Kidney problems, Low vitality and backache are associated with dysfunction of this chakra. Meng-mein is supposed to be a pumping station of energy in the spine for upward flow from Muladhara.

2. *Navel Chakra* controls small and large intestines and uterus (Womb).

   Constipation, appendicitis, difficult labour, low vitality are all associated with dysfunction of this chakra.

3. *Front Manipura Chakra* controls pancreas, liver, large intestine, appendix, stomach and diaphragm.

4. *Back Manipura Chakra* controls pancreas.

   Diabetes millitus, gallstones, peptic ulcer, rheumatoid arthritis are associated with dysfunction of these chakras. Manipura Chakra also controls the temperature regulating mechanism of the body and emotions (tension and stress).

   Malfunction of Manipura Chakra leads to malfunction of Anahata and Svadhishthana Chakras.

5. *Front Anahata Chakra* controls heart, thymus and circulatory system.

6. *Back Anahata Chakra* also controls heart, lungs and thymus. Always energize the heart from the back and never from the front.

7. *Forehead Chakra* controls central nervous system.

With this much general introduction of the Chakra System now we proceed to describe seven major Chakras in detail.

7

Muladhara (First) Chakra

(BASE/ROOT)

SUMMARY

Location: At the base of the backbone, near the tail.

Element: Earth

Color: Red

Sense: Smell

Development: From three months after the conception till adult life.

Nerve Plexus Influenced: Sacro coccygeal nerve plexus

Endocrine Glands Influenced: Adrenal glands

Organs/Systems Influenced: Digestive system (stomach and rectum), immune system, circulatory system, bone, muscles and connective tissue.

Mantra: Lam

Sound: Ohh

Functions: Rooting, Harmony with the Nature and laws of Nature, security, survival and expansion.

A Poorly Functioning Muladhara causes loss of trust in nature, focus on material possessions, need for satisfaction of desires, troubles, eating disorders, frequent illnesses due to poorly developed immune system and a weak musculoskeletal system.

An Over Functioning first chakra may cause overweight (obesity) due to overeating. It may also lead to greed, fear, non-security and addictions of various types.

Square represents four directions *i.e.*, east, west, north and south. Inverted triangle within arrow represents Susumana Nadi in the center and triangle pointing downwards represents that the first Chakra forces us down towards the earth. In the middle of the triangle there is Shiva-Lingam with Kundalini wrapped around it three and a half times.

The *elephant* represents heaviness of the chakra grounding towards the earth *i.e.*, root. Seven trunks of elephant represent seven pathways or connection of the first Chakra with the sixth Chakra.

In the *center of the square* is *Lam*, which is the seat sound of first Chakra. One can meditate on *Lam* to strengthen the first Chakra.

Muladhara Chakra is the lower most major chakra conforming to the foundation of the body, hence connecting the body to the Earth. This Chakra represents the present body with its past karmas.

TRADITIONAL VIEW

Muladhara, attached to the mouth of Susumana Nadi, is placed below genitalia and above Anus. It has four petals of crimson hue, these petals have four letters (*i.e.*, Va, Sa, Sa, Sa) and these letters are to be meditated upon. This Chakra is presided by Devi 'Dakini'. The Chakra is represented by a circle inside which is a square, which represents Earth. The square or the Earth has Bija of the Earth in the form of *Lam*, which is yellow in color. Inside this Bija is Indra sitting on the elephant. The Bija of the Earth has 'Brahma', the creator in its lap. Brahma here is described to have four arms, which means four Vedas. Here, Brahma as well as Devi 'Dakini' should be meditated upon.

Inside there is a triangle called 'Tripura' and Kundalini lies here because there is *Shiva-Linga* in the triangle and this Linga is placed on *Kama Bija*. Kundalini lies here wrapped up 3 times around the *Shiva-Linga*. She shines like lightning and is responsible for our breathing and is also the source of speech and poetry. She is *Maya*. She also represents *creation, existence* and *dissolution* and the *consciousness* itself. One should envisage Kundalini as a 16-year-old beautiful girl with restless eyes and should meditate upon her, because man becomes free of all sins by meditating upon Kundalini.

MODERN INTERPRETATION AND COMMENTS

In sanskrit Muladhara means root, and strong roots always give stability. Here, the roots represent our ancestry and our present make-up according to the karmas of our past lives. The karmas of our *pitras* (ancestors) are passed into our bodies through the genes.

Genes are being implicated in every sphere of our life and in coming years more diseases will be prevented/treated by modified genes. Modified genes will be able to modify the characteristics of individuals.

It has been learnt from the process of e.olution that survival instinct is the basis of our consciousness as inherited from our ancestors. As Darwin theory states, "the fittest survive and the rest perish". It is the fear of survival, which awakens the Muladhara Chakra, which in turn stimulates the adrenal glands. It leads to production of adrenalin (a hormone of adrenal glands) in larger quantities, which circulates in the blood stream giving the vital energy to the body for action. But chronic or constant *fear* keeps a permanent pressure on the mind which leads to chronic *stress*. Chronic stress puts further pressure on the vital organs of the body through nerves. Leading to weakness of those vital parts *i.e.*, pressure on the heart leads to heart disease and high blood pressure. Pressure on the gastrointestinal tract leads to chronic dyspepsia, formation of more acid in the stomach etc. Pressure on the mind and brain leads to insomnia (sleeplessness), chronic tiredness and depression etc.

Muladhara Chakra roots our bodies into the World and earth that is why it is said that we come out of the earth, the earth nourishes us and we go back to the Earth. The basic element of the Muladhara Chakra is the *earth*. If the earth (ground) below our feet is solid our roots are likely to be firm. This means if we are born in a family with stable background, if we have a caring mother, if we have been brought up in a loving family atmosphere then our roots are strong. Strong roots always nourish the tree of life which prospers as the time goes on and establishes the foundation for further growth. Weak roots mean improper nourishment, which makes the tree of life to collapse, which gives a sense of defeat to the body.

After having secured strong roots, constant and proper nourishment the tree of life wants to expand and this is the expansion, which creates faith in ourselves, gives us prosperity and independence. A normally functioning Muladhara Chakra achieves this all.

Another most important function of Muladhara Chakra is that this provides resting place to the Kundalini shakti, which lies dormant here. (Kundalini shakti is described in detail in a separate chapter.)

Muladhara Chakra strengthens the physical body, energizes muscles, bones including backbone and some internal organs. Without healthy first chakra we get trapped at the level of existence and survival, the progress and expansion are hampered as fear takes over.

A normal functioning Muladhara Chakra gives a sense of safety/security to the body which helps us in building our *Self-esteem*. It gives us the sense of well-being and this sense makes us progress further by improving our communication skills and making us develope faith and trust in others. Faith is a positive belief which means something good will come out of an action, whereas fear is a negative belief which means awful result of an action.

A traumatized and poorly functioning Muladhara Chakra ends up in weak foundation, lack of security, lack of confidence.

8

Svadhishthana (Second) Chakra

(SEX)

SUMMARY

Location: Perineum in the pelvic region behind genitalia.
Element: Water
Color: Orange
Sense: Taste
Development: From the age of nine months onwards.
Nerve Plexus Influenced: Lumbosacral nerve plexus.
Endocrine Gland Influenced: Testes in males and ovaries in female.
Organ/System Influenced: Kidneys, urinary bladder, reproductive organs and large intestine.
Mantra: Vam
Sound: Ooo
Functions: Center for sexual energy, source of pure emotions and regulator of relationships.
A Poorly Functioning Chakra leads to emotional instability, rigid attitudes and inability to express feelings.

Svadhishthana Chakra is represented by the lotus with six petals of red color, which also contains two more lotuses within it. At the base of the second lotus there is a moon-shaped crescent, which contains an animal called *makara*, which resembles a crocodile and represents consuming unwanted desire and passion, which are thought to be animal instincts. A channel on the top represents *Susumana Nadi* and two small circles in the inner lotus represent male and female energy. In the center, there is word *Wam*, which represents the seat sound of the chakra.

TRADITIONAL VIEW

This lotus has 6 petals, is situated in the perineum and is of vermillion color. Six petals have letters Ba, Bha, Ma, Ya, Ra and La. Inside the pericarp there is a 8 petaled lotus with a white center which is shaped like a half moon. Inside this is 'Varuna Bija' *Vam* seated on a Makara, in his lap is Vishnu seated on Garuda. Vishnu is youthful in appearance and has 4 arms and 4 hands holding *Conch, Discus, Mace* and *Lotus* in each hand. 'Shakti Rakani' is sitting besides Vishnu on a red lotus. She has four heads, three Eyes and Projecting Fangs and looks terrible to behold.

He who meditates on Svadhishthana is freed from all enemies *i.e., Passion, Greed, Anger, Ego, Attachment* etc. and comes out of ignorance.

MODERN INTERPRETATION AND COMMENTS

From rooting and grounding, instinct to survive, security and desire to expand, which are dealt with by Muladhara Chakra, we move upwards to further expansion in the form of growth of the body, growth of the mind, desire to attain knowledge (education) and desire to enjoy the pleasures of life, through sexual pleasure and procreation. All these are dealt with by Svadhishthana Chakra.

Svadhishthana means place or seat of taste. Taste depicts enjoyment. Greatest enjoyment in the life of a common human being comes from taste (eating) and sexuality (sexual pleasure). Svadhishthana Chakra starts developing between the ages of 6 months and 3 years and is situated (located) in the perineum in the pelvic region behind genitalia.

From element *earth,* which is solid and stable (Muladhara Chakra), we move on to Element *Water,* which is liquid and makes us move and flow forward (Svadhishthana Chakra). This flow helps us in strengthening different parts of the body. It also increases blood circulation in the body, stimulates the nervous system and gives vent to our feelings, which in turn help in developing our senses. Senses provide a link between the inside of the body with the outside world. By senses I mean *sight, sound, touch, hearing* and *taste.* These are the senses which make us capable of physical, emotional and spiritual experiences. Through our senses we form our basic beliefs and thought process. Senses make us differentiate between pleasure and pain, expansion and contraction and so many other things. Senses also make us aware of emotions, feelings, distinctions and values.

After having overcome survival, we focus on growth/ expansion, and growth of the body comes from the nourishment provided by the food. There comes a stage, when eating becomes a pleasure because pleasure takes the stress away, makes us relaxed and teaches us to live in the *present.* The same thing applies to sexuality. Outlet of sexual energy and emotions gives us pleasure by taking the stress away.

When pleasure is incomplete or denied, it makes us grow in the dark to find the way to complete pleasure. In this process, when we cannot find a proper way we feel insecure and become stubborn. The inborn pleasures or primary pleasures are: 'being wanted', 'being loved' and 'being respected'. When these primary pleasures are denied, the secondary pleasures like drinking, smoking, overeating and overindulgence in sex take over, which make us emotional, angry and depressed because emotions which rise from the subconscious take us away from harmful effects towards pleasure *i.e.,* instead of appreciating harmful effects of drinking, smoking, overeating and overindulgence in sex, we start deriving pleasure out of this activity. Emotions can be controlled/channelized by constant training and *pranayam* (control of breathing). The emotions can be let out/released by shouting, kicking, shaking and crying/sobbing. That is why listening to the loud music and shaking the body to the tune of that music is the best outlet for emotion. Desire is also an emotional impulse essential for the satisfaction of the senses.

There are some basic needs to maintain the body and these needs become *desire*. Desire is essential for progress and expansion; this is the seed of passion essential for developing energy to move forwards. It is the sense of guilt which hinders the free flow of energy forwards and allows the energies to accumulate ending up in dissatisfaction leading to compulsive repetitive acts ending up in compulsive disorders *e.g.*, compulsive eaters never feel satisfied and put on weight and lack of satisfaction makes them eat more forming a vicious circle.

Another important aspect, which is dealt by the Svadhishthana Chakra, is sexuality. Sexuality has always been misunderstood by the society because society has always created guilt in relation to sexuality, which becomes a direct hindrance to the pleasure. As a matter of fact, sexuality is the direct expression of emotions and desires leading to sensate pleasure. Sexuality being an important and burning topic of the day, I have taken the liberty of adding a separate chapter in this book in subsequent pages.

Sexual abuse hits this chakra hard and affects the free flow of energy depriving the individual of the pleasure, intimacy and emotions in the adult life. Hence, *rape* has a devastating effect on the Svadhishthana Chakra because this act is performed for power with violence, which affects the entire energy system.

Excessively energized Svadhishthana Chakra leads to intense emotional states, these people find it very difficult to be on their own and they are likely to depend on others for their social, sexual and emotional needs.

If depleted, Svadhishthana Chakra leads to restricted physical, emotional and sexual activity. There is a feeling of emptiness/dullness in life and person becomes isolated. The sexual feelings become suppressed or even non-existent leading to difficulty in arousal or attaining orgasm.

9

Manipura (Third) Chakra

(NAVEL)

SUMMARY

Location: At level of navel (belly-button).
Element: Fire
Color: Yellow
Sense: Sight
Development: From two years onwards.
Nerve Plexus Influenced: Solar plexus.
Endocrine Glands Influenced: Adrenal glands, liver and pancreas.
Organs/Systems Influenced: Pancreas, spleen, gall bladder, small intestines and sympathetic nervous system.
Mantra: Ram
Sound: Ahh
Functions: Tolerance, autonomy, self-esteem, power and ego identity.
A Poorly Functioning Manipura Chakra is represented by low energy, poor self-esteem, passiveness and non-reliability.
The center of this chakra is like a radiant jewel (gem).
Ten petals of lotus represent ten fingers of the hands. Hands have the ability to achieve any thing. Ten also

represents beginning of a new cycle and this chakra gives a new kind of awareness.

Within the lotus there is an inverted triangle which has incomplete Swastikas on each wall which represent the three gunas *i.e.*, sattvika, rajasika and tamasika. Within the lotus is an animal (Ram), which is a very energetic animal and is usually associated with agni (fire). When full of power this chakra represents male energy and when it is powerless it represents female energy.

TRADITIONAL VIEW

This is also called Nabhi Padma (Navel Lotus) because it is located at the level of belly-button. It has cloudy smoky color and the lotus has ten petals which have letters Da, Dha, Na, Ta, Tha, Da, Dha, Na, Pa, Pha on them. In the pericarp of lotus there is a red triangular region representing *Fire*. Within the triangular region is Bija of Fire 'Ram', which is seated on a *ram* and has four arms, holding Thunder Bolt and Shakti Weapons. In its lap is 'Rudra', who looks old and red in color and seated on a bull. Outside the triangle are three Svastika Signs.

In the pericarp is 'Shakti Lakini' seated on a red Lotus, she herself is blue in color and has three faces with three eyes on each face. She has four arms and her hands hold Shakti weapons. She has big projecting teeth and is fond of Meat and Blood. She dispels fears and grants Boons.

By meditating on Manipura Chakra, one acquires power to *Create* and *Destroy*.

MODERN INTERPRETATION AND COMMENTS

Earth (Muladhara Chakra) and *water* (Svadhishthana Chakra) are passive and move downward towards the gravity to follow the path of least resistance, but Manipura Chakra is represented by element fire, which rises upwards against the gravity, so that the energy reaches the upper chakras.

Manipura Chakra is situated in the center of the body at the level of the navel or belly-button. The element *fire* helps in digestion of food. Fire also means fire for liberation or fire for the name, fame and success. One has to decide whether one wants to set fire for name, fame and success or one wants to get consumed in the fire for liberation and attainment of the supreme, because one cannot achieve both the goals at a single given time.

The liberating current of energy rises upwards from first and second chakras, whereas energies from the upper chakras (chakras 6, 5 and 4) travel downwards and combination of these two energies at the third chakra manifest in the form of *power*. This is that power which is needed to confront the challenges.

Manipura means shining gem, the development of this chakra starts from the age of two years onwards.

Fire gives heat as well as light, hence it shows us the path to see and act in the journey from matter to consciousness.

To get connected to the universe at large, we need visualization, understanding and ways of communication, which are provided by the upper chakras, but before this we need to have a separate existence with autonomous individuality and to provide this, is the task of Manipura Chakra. Autonomy teaches us to take the responsibility of our actions, which gives us *power*. Carl Jung (a world renowned psychologist) called this autonomy as *individuation*, a journey towards awakening of the *ego*. That person who's Manipura Chakra does not get awakened, follows the path of least resistance and remains dependent throughout his life. Damage to first two chakras may also damage the third chakra. *Individuation* gives rise to ego, which is a conscious realization of ourselves as a separate entity. Considering ego as a very important subject in modern day and age, a separate chapter has been added to this book on this subject.

Power provided by the ego makes us transform ourselves, willing to make mistakes and accept responsibility for them to determine our *destiny*.

It is the shame, which subdues the power and makes us powerless. Shame makes us think that we are worthless and infuses a sense of inferiority in us. In other words, shame suppresses Manipura Chakra, whereas overactive third chakra infuses in us great excessive energy and greater power, which may end up in creating a false perception, such people keep themselves busy to accomplish certain goals to boost their ego. People with excessive energy in third chakra may abuse power and become highly strung and end up in developing dominating personalities.

Manipura Chakra weakens the ego and ends up in depression, feeling ashamed and avoiding confrontations. People with weak third chakra also suffer from chronic fatigue and get hooked on to stimulants like tea, coffee, alcohol and drugs. These addictions help them to lift their self-esteem (ego).

10

Ego

EGO is realization of the self and its capabilities. It gives us an individual identity and makes us master of our own will. In the society at large ego is considered synonymous with high headedness or stubbornness in day-to-day experience.

An egoist is a person who thinks of himself only and not of others; this is synonymous with *Egoism.* If Ego means "I", then egoism depends upon the relation between "I" and "no I", because Ego and Non-Ego go hand-in-hand and we cannot separate one from the other.

Ego coordinates the experiences of the first chakra *i.e.,* internal world and second chakra *i.e.,* external world into the third chakra. Ego is combination of energies coming from upper Chakras as well as from lower chakras. It works as an executive identity of the self and tells us as well as others who we are? And what we are?

As we get older and leave our childhood behind, we grope in search of individuality and autonomy, because autonomy is essential for taking responsibility of our own actions. Autonomy brings *power* with it. In Carl Jung's words, this is called *individuation* and an individuation gives rise to ego. In other words, ego is realization of ourselves as a separate identity, master of its own, which operates the self. A strong ego is able to integrate bad/difficult experiences, so as to maintain the functioning of the Self.

The word *EGO* comes from Greek, where 'E' stands for 'I' and 'go' stands for 'Earth', which means, 'I stand on my own ground'. Ego is conscious element of self, but it does not include our unconscious hopes, dreams and fears etc.

Ego channelizes our energy towards a goal. Ego can unite as well as divide, and is necessary for attainment of individuality. Ego gives us a place to grow, to change and to expand, hence is essential for the development of our personality within prescribed limits/boundaries.

Many religious disciplines advise us to give up ego, considering it as bad or false, but this is not true. Because of its boundaries ego is self-limiting and we stay within those confines, because of fear, guilt or shame and never get out of it. It is not wrong to have boundaries but those should not create any limitations, rather those should be for new experiences. Without ego we cannot expand and with expansion we show our power/self-esteem. People with high self-esteem are more capable of taking care of themselves and Manipura Chakra provides all this energy.

We must have a strong ego and abide by it because without ego our progress is hampered.

If ego is 'I' and when 'I' is gone, nothing is left.

Ego gives birth to desire and desire produces envy, malice, jealousy, hatred and so forth. This is the desire, which gives bad name to the ego. There are three degrees in egoism:

1. What we are *i.e.*, our body and our life.
2. What we have *i.e.*, our wealth, property and other possessions.
3. What we represent *i.e.*, honor, rank, name, fame etc.

The invasion of these three territories leads to wickedness.

The yoga teaches us that when the sense of limitation is removed by divine consciousness, we shed our ego.

11

Anahata (Fourth) Chakra
(HEART)

SUMMARY

Location: In the chest, near the heart.
Element: Air
Color: Green
Sense: Touch
Development: From the age of four years onwards.
Nervous Plexus Influenced: Cardiac plexus
Endocrine Glands Influenced: Thymus
Organs/Systems Influenced: Heart, lungs, blood circulation and vagus nerves.
Mantra: Yam
Sound: Ayy
Functions: Love, relationships, intimacy and devotion. Here feelings are converted into emotions and negative feelings are neutralised.
A Poorly Functioning Anahata Chakra leads to loneliness, self-criticism, fear of relationship, isolation and non-acceptance of love given by others.

Anahata means *sound* and this is unstuck sound made without striking two things. It is represented by a lotus of twelve petals, inside which are two triangles, one with the apex upwards (representing Male energy) and other with the apex downwards (representing Female energy).

Twelve petals represent male and female energy in six petals each and depict union of these two energies.

Two triangles represent descent of spirit in the body and ascent of matter rising to meet the spirit. In the center, the word *Yam* represents the mantra of this chakra.

TRADITIONAL VIEW

This lotus with 12 petals and of vermilion color is situated in the region of the heart, where a sound is produced unstuck. Twelve petals have letters from 'Ka to Tha'. In the pericarp of the lotus is the 'Vayu Mandal' of smoky hue. Above this is 'Surya Mandal', which is triangular in shape and very bright in color. Above which is the Vayu Bija of smoky hue, which is seated on a black antelope, which has four arms. In the lap of the Vayu Bija is the three-eyed 'Isa'.

In the pericarp of the lotus is seated Shakti 'Kakini' on a red lotus, she has four arms and carries Noose, Skull, Vara and Abhaya Signs. She is golden in color and has a garland of Skulls around her neck. Her heart is full of nectar.

In the middle of the triangle is 'Shiva', in the form of Bana Linga. He is happy with desire and below him is 'Jivatma' like 'Hamsa'.

Below the pericarp of this lotus is 8 petalled red lotus, which has 'Kalpa tree', the Jewelled altar and this is the place of mental worship.

A yogi is capable of Dhyana and Avadhana (intense concentration).

A person, who meditates on this Chakra is dear to women, he is full of noble deeds. He has all his senses under control. His speech is fluent and clear. He is a *Devta*, who is beloved of *Laxmi* and is able to enter another body at his *Will*.

MODERN INTERPRETATION AND COMMENTS

After developing individuality, self-esteem and ego,

provided by Manipura Chakra, the energy ascends up in search of love, which is the inborn right of every individual, to Anahata Chakra, which is located in the region of the heart near the cardiac plexus.

The element of this chakra is air and the fire brought from Manipura Chakra gets fanned in Anahata Chakra, the development of which starts from the age of four years onwards.

Anahata means *unstuck*, that means a sound produced without striking two things. Heart muscle is an involuntary muscle, hence its contraction and relaxation is not within the control of our *will.* The sound produced by the heartbeat is unstuck.

To love and to be loved is the basic right of Heart Chakra. It is the love, which guides our lives, creates and holds relationships and liberates our energy. Love makes everything look bright by creating strong connections and making us feel secure.

Air, which is element of this chakra means coolness and expansion. Hence, love expands to the limits that it can take the whole universe in stride. Love awakens ourselves towards spirituality and becomes the greatest binding force between different individuals *i.e.*, man and man or man and woman or even between individual and God.

The energy coming from lower chakras binds the body, whereas energy coming from upper chakras liberates the soul. These two energies come to a perfect balance at Anahata Chakra, where it enters the realms of love and this balance creates equilibrium between love and relationship. Relationship does not only mean a relationship between two individuals but it also means relationship between body and soul, because before loving another individual we need to love ourselves. If we are in love with ourselves, then we need to be on our own so as to enjoy our own company.

Anahata Chakra is the place where we create a balance of our own energies (male as well as female aspect of energy) *i.e.*, Shiva and Shakti. This balance is also very important in personal relationships, whether these are at home or at work place or those are social or sexual relationships. Lack of this balance creates stress and frustrations leading to failure of relationships.

A failed relationship invariably ends up in *grief.*

In grief, the anahata chakra shuts down, making a person feel dead inside and rejected. As it is said rightly that time is the best healer, with time and sympathies of near and dears the Heart Chakra starts opening up gradually.

The energy, which comes from upper chakras to Anahata Chakra, brings a sense of compassion as well as a feeling of devotion. Compassion is a perfect balance between upper and lower chakra expression represented by selfless action, whereas devotion is an act of selfless love and surrender to the universal force/energy. All world religions teach devotion because devotion is an act of egoless surrender, without any questions being asked.

Rejection is the biggest fear for the Heart Chakra because it is the fear of rejection, which makes us hold back our love and blocks this chakra, but rejection also makes us realize the truth that we need to face a change.

Excessive energy in Anahata Chakra may lead to excessive love for the others or God, to the extent that it may become an obsession leading to our own insecurity because addiction to anything undermines our clarity and judgment.

Deficiency of energy in Anahata Chakra creates wounds in love, we feel guilty of loosing our lover, we also feel angry and betrayed and are not willing to forgive and forget and this makes us judgmental and less compassionate.

A lonely Heart Chakra is always ready to open up again.

12

Vishuddha (Fifth) Chakra

(SOUND)

SUMMARY

Location: Neck, at the level of the throat.

Element: Sound (Air)

Color: Blue

Sense: Speech and Hearing.

Development: Starts between the age of 7 to 12 years.

Nerve Plexus Influenced: Laryngeal plexus

Endocrine Glands Influenced: Thyroid and para-thyroid glands.

Organs/System Influenced: Larynx, respiratory system and vagus nerves.

Mantra: Ham

Sound: Eeee

Functions: Communication, expression of emotions and inner reflection.

A Poorly Functioning Vishuddha Chakra leads to lack of expression, husky voice, introversion, fear of silence and fear of being rejected.

Vishuddha means 'purification'. To open this chakra body must reach certain purification by vibrations (sound), which is present in all things and has a purifying nature.

Vishuddha (fifth) Chakra is represented by a circle, which

has an inverted triangle inside, and photograph of a white elephant in the center. There is word *Ham*. The elephant in the inverted triangle symbolizes the manifestation of speech and the whole star represents full moon.

Element of this Chakra is *air*, associated element is *ether* or *akasha*, which gives awareness to perceive the field of vibration, known as *etheric plane* and this plane can manifest the super-normal phenomenon *i.e.*, remote viewing, remote healing, telepathy etc.

Diseases usually manifest in the etheric body first, before going to the physical body. Acupuncture, homoeopathy, pranic healing and psychic healing are all done at etheric body level.

TRADITIONAL VIEW

This purple colored lotus is situated at the level of the throat and has 16 petals, which are 16 *Vowels* red in color.

In its pericarp is ethereal region, which is a white circle, inside which is 'Bija Ham'. This Bija is white in color and is seated on an elephant, which has four arms. In the lap of the Bija is 'Sada Shiva' seated on a loin seat, which is placed on a bull. Shiva's half body is golden and the other half is snow white. He has five faces and ten arms. He holds Trident, Battle Axe, Sword, Thunder Bolt, Great Snake, Bell, Goad and Noose. He wears a tiger skin and his whole body is smeared with ashes, he has Garland of snakes around his neck. The nectar is dropping on his forehead.

Within the pericarp and in the Lunar region is 'Shakti Sakini' seated on bones. She has four arms, five faces and three eyes, carrying in her hands a bow, an arrow, a noose and a goad.

He, who has attained a comprehensive knowledge of *Soul*, becomes a great sage by meditating on this Chakra and attains peace of mind. He becomes free from disease and sorrow and enjoys a long life.

Meditation on this Chakra destroys endless dangers.

MODERN INTERPRETATION AND COMMENTS

After traversing the realms of love, compassion and devotion (Anahata Chakra), the energy moves up to Vishuddha Chakra, which acts as a filter and resonator for the energy to ascend up. Shuddha means pure and Vishuddha means center for purification, so the energy is filtered at Vishuddha Chakra and pure form of energy ascends upwards towards Ajna Chakra. This chakra also influences the lower chakra.

Vishuddha Chakra is situated at the level of the throat in the neck. Its development starts between the ages of 7 and 12 years depending upon the development of the lower chakras.

Muladhara deals with *form*, Svadhishthana deals with *Movement*, Manipura deals with *Activity* and Anahata deals with *Love and Relationship*. From here the Vishuddha Chakra takes over to give *vibration and phonation* (resonance) to the energy. Resonance means rhythm and it is a very common saying *My life is out of rhythm* or *My body rhythm is good today.* In modern times, people sway their bodies with the rhythm of the music so that rhythm of the music and body gets synchronized. Resonance/vibrations are already present in the energy vital for the body. The job of Vishuddha Chakra is to enhance this resonance. When this resonance is low, we feel uncomfortable and uneasy. This resonance of the vital energy connects the body with the mind, which reflects the state of our health and amount of vitality in our body. If we wish to resonate with the world around us, we have to adjust the wavelength of the resonance of our body and mind with the wavelength of the energy of the world around us.

If there is too much resonance/vibration in our body, we are likely to get tired very soon. It is the sleep, which usually puts us back in harmony with our own resonance.

Vibrations also give rise to sound *i.e.*, phonation and this is the job of Vishuddha Chakra to give energy to our sound box to be expressed as speech, which is the best form of communication/self-expression with the outside world.

Neck (Throat) acts as a bottleneck for the passage of energies upwards; hence Vishuddha Chakra acts as a filter between body and the mind, because as soon as we pass above the neck we reach the domain of the brain where the mind resides. But the mind can only interpret those things of which it has the knowledge before. So Vishuddha Chakra acts as the relay system for the messages from the body and connects this with the information already stored in the brain. It also acts as a filter to make sure that only purified energy reaches the Agya (Ajna) Chakra. To enter the world of mind some sort of *symbols* are essential, because these symbols represent our past experiences. A symbol speaks when it has a meaning and our body resonates with it.

(Symbols are dealt with in detail in the chapter of Ajna Chakra).

Vishuddha Chakra supplies energy to our *voice box* and that energy is expressed in the form of *voice*. So the pitch or the intensity of the voice depends on the amount of energy present in the Vishuddha Chakra. If this chakra is healthy the voice is resonant and rhythmic and conversation becomes a balanced act between the speaker and the listener.

As a matter of fact almost all chakras influence our voice.

○ A poorly developed first Chakra *restricts* the voice.
○ A malfunctioning second Chakra makes the voice *mechanical.*
○ A constricted third Chakra makes the voice *pinched.*
○ A disturbed fourth Chakra reduces the *intensity* of the voice.
○ A restricted fifth Chakra changes the voice into a *whisper.*
○ A closed sixth Chakra makes the voice *dull and repetitive.*

It is the integration of various voices in the body, which create resonance, and communication is the expression of that resonance, which takes place at the level of the Vishuddha Chakra. Hence, voice is the living expression of our basic vibrations. *Fear* and *anger* choke the fifth chakra and prolonged fear closes it down. *Guilt and shame* also affect Vishuddha Chakra, leading to lack of expression of our feelings. Telling lies, screaming/shouting etc. also affect the fifth chakra, because lying creates a sense of guilt and shame.

Deficiency of energy in Vishuddha Chakra leads to weak or pinched voice and incoherent speech which is unable to find a proper expression, whereas excessive energy in the fifth chakra gives control of the rhythm in voice and conversation, and makes the speech beautiful.

13

Ajna (Sixth) Chakra

(THIRD EYE)

SUMMARY

Location: Glebella (area of the forehead between eyebrow).

Element: Light (cosmic light), Ether.

Color: Indigo

Sense: Sixth sense

Development: From puberty onwards.

Nerve Plexus/Part of the Brain: Cerebellum and its lobes.

Endocrine Gland Influence: Pituitary gland, hypothalamus, and Pineal gland.

Organ/Systems Influenced: Hind brain, left eye and nose.

Mantra: OM

Sound: Mmm

Functions: Pattern recognition, connection to the rest of the creation, intuition, dreams, visualization and imagination.

A Poorly Functioning Ajna Chakra leads to lack of imagination, poor memory, difficulty in visualization, non-remembrance of dreams and afraid of intuition.

Ajna Chakra is represented by two petals of Lotus, which may represent meeting of two nadis *ida* and *pingla.* Since the petals are shaped like wings and symbolize that this chakra can transcend time and space allowing the inner spirit to distant time and places. The corresponding element of this Chakra is *light* and light gives us the information. How much we are able to see depends upon the development and openness of Ajna Chakra, which includes normal eyesight. This chakra gifts a person with psychic perceptions like seeing an aura or details of astral plane and remote viewing *i.e.*, seeing things at other places.

This Chakra being situated in the head area is related to pineal gland, which is situated in the brain. Pineal gland is also called the 'seat of the soul', which translates vibrations into hormonal messages relayed to the body through nervous system. *Pineal gland* reaches the height of its development around the age of nine and influences the maturation of the sex glands. In the early stage of development the pineal gland is situated at the level of the third eye, which changes its position inwards as the foetus grows. Pineal gland produces a hormone called *melatonin*. Melatonin production decreases with the advancing age. Melatonin has been used as a sleeping agent particularly during *jetlag*. It increases dreaming, showing that melatonin has some relevance to inner vision. Some psychotropic drugs like LSD increase melatonin production; hence trigger the phenomenon of inner vision that is why people get addicted to these drugs.

As explained earlier pineal gland is supposed to control the function of the pituitary gland and pituitary gland is supposed to be king of all endocrine glands. The pituitary by its hormones is responsible for growth, metabolism, physical activity and sexual activity of a person. As long as pineal gland remains active and intact it controls the pituitary *i.e.*, pineal is master and pituitary is subordinate. With the advancing age the relationship of pineal and pituitary glands are reversed and one becomes prone to all sort of mental and physical problems.

It is the functions of the pineal gland which are linked with the phenomenon of telepathy. It's a traditional thinking that by concentrating/meditating on the Ajna Chakra one can get rid of all the bad karmas of the past lives. It is here that the yogis concentrate their energy at the time of *samadhi*.

TRADITIONAL VIEW

Lotus of this Chakra has two petals, which are white in color and have letters *Ha* and *Ksa* on them. This Chakra is located on the forehead in between the two eyebrows, it is also called third eye or eye of wisdom.

'Shakti Hakim' is in the pericarp of the lotus. She has six faces, each face has three eyes, six arms and is seated on a white lotus. In her hands she holds Rudraksha rosary, a human skull, a drum and a book. Above her is located 'Itra Linga' in a triangle, above which is *Antaratma* (Supreme Soul) like a flame. Above this is Manas in the region of the moon within whom is 'Param Shiva and his Shakti'. This Chakra is abode of 'Vishnu'.

A good Yogi, at the time of death places his *Prana* at this Chakra and enters eternal and birthless worlds.

MODERN INTERPRETATION AND COMMENTS

Energy after getting filtered at the level of Vishuddha Chakra moves upwards to Ajna (agya) Chakra, which is situated on the forehead in between the two eyebrows and is also called *third eye*. This chakra acts as an inner eye and interprets the objects seen by the physical eyes in the light of memory, past experiences, imagination and intuition.

This is the *third eye* where Shiva resides in the form of refined Male energy and when the crude and rough, Female energy (Shakti) combines with this, it creates an enlightening and liberating energy, which transcends.

The element of this chakra is light, which means when you come from darkness to light, you start seeing clearly, even the distant objects become visible. Agya Chakra shapes the energy brought from other chakras in the form of information. These shapes are converted into particular patterns, which get stored in the memory. Pattern reorganization requires the ability to see into present, past and future, which is provided by Ajna or Agya Chakra.

Agya means *to order* (or command) and Ajna means *to perceive*. This chakra orders the energy to be perceived in different patterns according to past experiences/karmas. In other words, Ajna Chakra makes us perceive our original identity. Original identity is the basic foundation of religion and mythology and opens doors for us to the spiritual identity and that door is between sixth and seventh Chakra.

Symbols (patterns) represent our original identity. We visualize the symbols, see them in dreams, fantasise them, wear them, draw them on paper or cloth or metal etc., decorate our homes with them and ultimately establish a spiritual communication with them. These focusing devices infused with spirituality are called *Yantras*. Realizing the importance of yantras, a full chapter has been added to this book on this subject.

Most important source of these symbols are our dreams, because dreams link the conscious mind (sixth and seventh chakras) with unconscious mind (lower chakras). Dreams reveal our hidden feelings, desires and needs and even provide answers for them. Prophet Mohammed visualized *Allah* in his dream only. Dreams link everyday experiences with spiritual experience and these are all represented by symbols, which are interpreted by intuition and Ajna Chakra again provides this intuitional energy.

Intuition is unconscious reorganization of a pattern and is not under the control of our will. Intuition increases our psychic ability to understand the cosmic world.

The ability to perceive or visualize certain things, which cannot be perceived by a normal individual is called *clairvoyance*. These people develop extra sensory perception and abilities to see into the past or future, to forecast the coming events to visualize the auras and chakras. Clear mind means clear vision, which can see and feel shapes and images in the light provided by Ajna Chakra. When a person can hear the coming events or the voices of the *spirits* etc., it is called *clairaudience*, again this ability is provided by the fifth chakra.

Agya Chakra also makes us *self-centered*, rather than *ego-centered*. Self-centering means trying to obtain knowledge of the self or wholeness and our relationship with the cosmic energy. Dreams, symbols, intuitions and images lead us to vision of ourselves, because once we can understand ourselves, we can try to find our relationship with the world around us in a more deeper sense.

Vision shows us the path to the future and liberates us from the past and this vision is provided by the third eye, which also visualizes pattern. Pattern reveals the identity of a particular item and once that identity is established the third eye makes us see beyond into the depth of the pattern.

A fully energized Ajna Chakra makes us multi sensory individuals. A person with highly developed Ajna Chakra is supposed to have a sixth sense, because Ajna Chakra is the sixth chakra. A normal human being is a five-sense human being, other senses are higher senses and this is the Ajna Chakra, which makes us aware of the other senses. Multi-sensory humans like Krishna, Buddha and Christ had exceptionally overdeveloped Ajna Chakras.

Underdeveloped Ajna Chakra ends up in mental blindness. These people prefer to be left alone, they do not like the change, they prefer the way they are and remain deprived of spiritualism.

An excessively energized Ajna Chakra in a normal human being leads to obsessional states, hallucinations (false visual perceptions), delusions (false auditory perceptions); these are all classed under psychotic disorders.

14

Kundalini Shakti

Kundalini represents the physical form of the energy, which becomes source of all our experiences. Kundalini is a force, which is distinct from prana, which may be called vitality or life principal. This is the energy, which makes us breathe hence it is 'Prana Devata'.

In Carl Jung's words, *"Kundalini is that indwelling energy which by self-identification with your opinions and character traits preserves your identity"*.

Ego in Sanskrit is called *Ahamkar*. This ego is the force which makes us accept the word as it is; the same force is called *Kundalini* when it is turned towards spiritualism. After kundalini is awakened it becomes very difficult, rather impossible to believe the worldly reality (external reality) as the sole reality.

Kundalini cannot be understood, it can only be experienced. A spiritual awakening altogether changes the way an individual experiences in this world.

To understand kundalini fully, one should try to understand *Tantra* first. Tantra is not a religion. A tantric believes in truth and reality that all of us are a part of manifested universe, subject to its laws, unless we develop the power to redefine ourselves. The aim of the tantric is to become self-functioning and to be free of all the limitations. Tantra is the living wisdom, which must be obtained from an experienced practitioner (guru). Our body is made of 5 elements (*tattva*) and essence of Tantra is to purify these five elements to awaken the Kundalini Shakti.

As mentioned earlier Kundalini Shakti identifies with the body, it represents 'Self-Identity' (ego), and resides/stays in the lower most chakra (Muladhara Chakra) situated at the base of the spine (backbone). Due to gravity it remains asleep there in ignorance. As soon as Kundalini (Kundalini is represented as *Shakti*) is awakened it strives to travel upwards to be liberated. You can liberate this ego by counteracting the force of gravity by penance. The purpose is to disengage the ego from her identification with the limited personality, so that she may unite with her perennial personality. The Ego has a strong grip on the body and it is not easy to rip it off. Some people die of shock when kundalini is awakened.

Kundalini is identified with maya (*Prakriti*). Ego is purest of the energies (shakti), but lies dormant under the cover of:

(a) *Gunas* (sattva, rajas and tamas).
(b) *Senses* particularly sense of taste; there are six tastes *i.e.*, sweet, sour, salty, bitter, spicy and pungent.
(c) *Five elements i.e.*, earth, water, air, fire and ether.

Gunas control the mind, elements shape the body and tastes control our internal chemistry, which link the body and mind. All these three things distort the human consciousness.

In kundalini yoga (raising of kundalini), we begin with purification of five elements, so as to allow the kundalini to travel upwards through different chakras. Force of her motion, if unimpeded, lifts the other coverings and produces spiritual wisdom. After three coverings are removed kundalini becomes naked and this withdraws the mind from external senses and takes it towards internal orgasm.

Kundalini can only be raised by control of prana

(pranayama). In pranayama, the energy takes two routes — the energy which moves upwards is called *Prana* and the energy which moves downwards is called *Apana*.

To raise the Kundalini one has to move prana downwards and apana upwards. When a proper balance is produced between apana and prana, kundalini starts rising from Muladhara Chakra. It throws up all its connections with the element earth, which includes greed and emotions based in muladhara and becomes free of the hold of solid element Earth.

When kundalini leaves Svadhishthana, the seat of element water and procreation, it leaves the person with the full knowledge of water element, he conquers lust and the drive to procreate.

The Manipura Chakra represents fire, hence metabolism. Manipura Chakra converts the Fire to satisfy hunger, into the fire to attain spiritualism or knowledge of the supreme. If too much energy is taken in and is not converted into hunger for knowledge, it gets converted into *Anger* which is a creation of element fire. This anger happens due to indigestion of the energy and this indigestion takes place if there is element of *doubt*; these doubts can only be removed by experience.

When there is too much energy in the system and it cannot be assimilated rightly, then it leads to certain mental problems and magnification of attachments. Here in this chakra the kundalini gets refined and this refined energy moves up to Anahata Chakra.

From Manipura Chakra kundalini moves up to Anahata Chakra to meet the element air; here it expands. This chakra is meant for sacrifices or performing of auspicious acts. 'Anahata' means 'unstuck'. Next to this chakra is heart which produces sound in the air and one develops comprehension.

From Anahata Chakra, kundalini moves up to Vishuddha Chakra, which means *Pure* and this gives knowledge of element ether, purest of the five elements.

After crossing this chakra, kundalini gets above all the five elements; here only three Gunas remain to obscure the kundalini. At the level of this chakra the breath becomes calm and regular and yogis practise *pranayama*, because control of breath calms the mind, which becomes easy to control. In turn, controlled mind controls breathing, hence mind becomes conditioned.

From this controlled mind the kundalini moves up to Ajna (agya) Chakra. This is a two-petalled chakra, hence has two bija mantras, one for Shakti (female) and other for Shiva (male). Ajna means 'command' and it is shiva who commands. At Ajna Chakra breathing stops and a zero state exists, which means all names and forms disappear and one is only aware of ones own individuality; everything in universe becomes unmanifested and cannot be perceived.

Kundalini becomes free from the bondage of the karmas beyond five elements. Here, the Kundalini (shakti) unites with the Shiva and this reunion creates half male and half female energy (the enlightened one). This enlightened energy arises up to Sahasrara (crown) Chakra as a single energy. Before reaching Sahasrara Chakra this energy travels through *golata, lalata and lalana chakras* (situated inside the brain), where it is converted into *Amrita*, which from Sahasrara trickles downwards and permeates the entire body with the supreme bliss.

So long kundalini remains confined to lower chakras (Chakras 1, 2, 3), there is danger of self-identification with the body; but once it rises above Vishuddha Chakra (chakra 4), one becomes free from karmic debts and no physical ties remain. Once kundalini reaches Sahasrara Chakra (chakra 7), it completely merges with the universal soul (universal cosmic energy).

Once kundalini is free from all bondage, it can travel up and down (upper chakras or lower chakras), without getting affected. Job of the kundalini shakti is realization of supreme consciousness by taking the form of the Goddess.

15

Sahasrara (Seventh) Chakra
(CROWN CHAKRA)

SUMMARY

Location: At the top of the head.

Element: Through process (ether).

Color: Violet to white (violet from human side and white from cosmic side).

Sense: Super sense

Development: From adulthood onwards.

Nerve Plexus/Part of Brain influenced: Right and left cerebral hemispheres, corpus colosum (Part of the brain joining right and left cerebral hemispheres.

Endocrine Glands Influenced: Pineal gland, thalamus and hypothalamus.

Organs/System Influenced: Higher brain and right eye.

Mantra: Mantras of individual deities/Gayatri mantra.

Sound: Nugg

Functions: Universal identity, spirituality, divinity and union with the supreme energy.

Poorly Functioning Seventh Chakra: Spiritual cynicism, rigid beliefs and learning difficulties.

TRADITIONAL VIEW

Above all the Chakras, within the Susumana Nadi and below
Visarga is this thousand petalled lotus, which is shining,
whiter and brighter than a full moon. The petals of the lotus
are turned downwards and tinged with golden color of the
sun; its body is luminous with letters beginning with A.

Within Sahasrara is full moon in a clear sky, whose eyes are
shining, moist and cool like nectar.

There is an empty triangular area, which is served in secret
by all "Suras" (Demons).

Yogi who has controlled his mind has known this Chakra,
gets free of all bondage of birth and death (Moksha). He can
do all, what he wishes. His speech is pure and sweet.

MODERN VIEW AND COMMENTARY

Energy in its crude form, which started from Muladhara
Chakra, got gradually refined as it passed through
Svadhishthana, Manipura and Anahata Chakras was filtered
at Vishuddha Chakra, unites with universal wisdom of
Shiva at Ajna Chakra. Having attained wisdom and insight,
realizing supernatural powers, this monoeistic energy which
cannot differentiate between male and female or between
good and bad or between I and you, moves upwards to
Sahasrara Chakra, which is not a Chakra in true sense. But it
is situated outside the domain of the bio-plasmic body above
the head. This chakra opens up like a thousand-petalled
Lotus towards the cosmos. The energy tries to get out of this
chakra to establish its connection with its mother *i.e.*, the
universal cosmic energy.

The final destination of the human race is to identify the
soul, which is a part of cosmic energy, find its relationship
with the body and its functions and ultimately to find ways
and means by which it can go and unite with its mother, after
having fulfilled its purpose.

By opening the Sahasrara (crown) Chakra, we open the floodgates to universal consciousness and this can be done through spiritual education, spiritual experiences and meditation, and by attaining a state of complete detachment. The worldly relations created by prakriti are forgotten and a relationship with the supreme is established, through devotion, belief and single directional mind. The images, which originated in the Ajna Chakra become responsible for the generation of our beliefs. As the inner awareness takes place we start forgetting the outside world. The inner awakening makes us discover the universe and we try to locate our identity in relation to the universe.

Meditation and spiritual experiences break our bonds with lower 'worldly' identities and establish the bond with the universal identity and these bonds get converted into beliefs. In universal identity, we visualize the cosmos and leave our worldly attachments. There is no need to lose our personal (ego) identity when we identify ourselves with the supreme, because the supreme identity becomes far more stable when our lower needs are satisfied.

Here I would like to refer to attachment and expectations, which are the bases of all suffering, unfortunately these are very much interwoven in our lives. We get attached to our children, parents, beloved, our goals, our beliefs etc. Attachment takes our energy away from ourselves and focuses it somewhere else, whereas it is important to focus our energy on ourselves. Attachments lead to expectations and if expectations remain unfulfilled it further leads to frustrations. By surrendering our attachments, we can experience our identity with the supreme, and this surrender does not require us to relinquish our lower states. By surrendering, we feel liberated *i.e.*, free from limitations of the mind and the outside world.

This (Seventh Chakra) provides a door between the outside infinite cosmic world and inside world of vision, imagination, creation and manifestation. By reaching infinite our limitations are taken away, whereas by looking inside makes us realize the divinity within ourselves in its wholeness. In the words of Ramakrishna, "Musk forms in the navel of the deer and gives a very maddening fragrance. Fascinated with fragrance the deer runs here, there and everywhere, to find the source of the smell, not realizing that it is coming from his own body. Likewise, God (the supreme) resides in the human body, not realizing that, the humans search for this everywhere else except within themselves".

Ultimate realization is not to connect with the divine, but to become divine. The merging of consciousness with the omnipresent is a state of enlightenment, which is attained by very few, but for most of us it is far beyond even to have a glimpse of it.

The individuals in which the Sahasrara (Crown) Chakra does not get opened cannot realize the God. These trapped energies may either get fixed at a single point leading to the criticism of the self or these energies take a repetitive pattern in our lives to reach our consciousness. One may get trapped in wrong beliefs always thinking about the negative side of every act.

Excessive energy in Crown Chakra may lead to spiritual addictions, arresting the growth in other directions.

A chronic excess of energy in upper Chakras (Chakras 5, 6 and 7) may lead to development of neurotic and psychotic disturbances. Psychosis manifests as hallucinations or delusions and neurosis leads to obsessional repetitive states.

16

Summary of Chakra Functions

Sahasrara (crown) Chakra identifies with the universal cosmic energy or creation and ends up in liberation from bondage and ignorance. Here the Astral Plane ends.

Ajna or Agya Chakra orders us to analyse ourselves helps in development of intuition, self-realization and transcendence.

Vishuddha (fifth) Chakra gives one creative identity, communication and self-expression. It also makes one hear heavenly voices and music (Clareaudience).

Anahata (fourth) Chakra moves one into social identity, relationships, love for humans as well as the supreme, intimacy and compassion. It makes one aware of joys and sorrow of others.

Manipura (third) Chakra brings in ego identity, self-esteem and power. One becomes partially aware of Astral journeys like a sensation of flying through the air.

Svadhishthana (second) Chakra gives us emotional identity and sexual identity. One becomes conscious in the physical body of the vague astral influences, which may be friendly or hostile.

Muladhara (first) Chakra identifies us with the self *i.e.*, body its identity and needs, one's past karmas. Here one begins to live at "Astral Plane".

17

Universal Energy Field

Brahma is super consciousness (Energy) and since we are *Brahma*, we are molecules of highest form of energy called 'Par-brahma'.

This Par-brahma is synonymous with the *universal energy field*. The whole universe is an energy field and everything in this field is connected or a part of it. The universal energy field is not limited to our galaxy (milky way) rather all the galaxies are connected with one another through this energy field.

This universal energy field is the highest and largest form of energy and everything else in the universe is a tiny part of it.

Since spirit or atma is a part of this energy, after the death of the physical body this (atma) energy goes and joins with the mother energy and from the mother energy another energy is created.

There has been a controversy for a long time between matter and energy. Recently scientists have proved that all stones (which are thought to be solid form of matter) have electro-magnetic energy at the subatomic level. Hence, it proves that everything in this universe is nothing but a form of energy.

18

Sources of Human (Vital) Energy

So far, we have explained the pattern of the energy inside the human body and how that energy is distributed and helps in functioning of the normal healthy body.

We will now explain how and from where the body gets this energy. Basically, the human body derives its energy from the *Universal Energy*. Universal energy itself comes from the three sources: (1) Sun, (2) Cosmos, and (3) Earth — with its electro-magnetic field.

(1) *Sun:* Sun is the source of energy to the whole galaxy, this gives energy in the form of heat as well as light, and without this energy survival is impossible. Sun not only gives energy to the planet earth, but also it energizes various other planets including Moon, which is the satellite of planet Earth.

(2) *Cosmos:* To define cosmos is not an easy job. It has been proved by the astronomers that cosmos is a sallicial bomb of energy in which various gases are being burnt at a very high speed producing unimaginable energy, which is distributed to all the galaxies, although we are only aware of our own galaxy called 'milky way'. We do not know, how many other galaxies exist in the Universe.

Besides Sun and other unknown sources, the major contributors to the cosmic energy are planets and various stars. The known planets are Moon (in reality Moon is the satellite of Earth), Mars, Mercury, Jupiter, Venus, Saturn, Neptune, Uranus and Pluto. And out of these planets Moon is nearest to Earth, next come Mercury and Venus. Next to Venus is Sun and on the other side of the Sun are Mars, Jupiter and Saturn. Neptune, Uranus and Pluto are still farther away.

These planets, like Earth, have tremendous resources of energy in the form of various gases, electro-magnetic waves and other radioactive waves etc. These planets and various other stars not only contribute energy to the cosmos but have a direct effect on the body and mind of each and every individual.

According to vedic astrology, all the planets have a direct effect on the functioning of human body and their attainments. There are certain planets, the energies of which give profitable and good effects, like Moon, Jupiter, Venus and Mercury, whereas energies of Saturn and Mars are considered to be not very helpful to human beings. I do not wish to get into controversy of astrology. Here our purpose is to make the reader aware of the sources from which the energy is accumulated in cosmos and planets are the major contributors.

3. *Earth:* This is one of the biggest sources of energy for the inhabitants of this planet because all the food grows from Earth, which is necessary for the survival of the inhabitants. Various plants and trees grow on the Earth which in the presence of Sun energy give out oxygen and imbibe carbon-dioxide and this is the oxygen which is an essential constituent of *prana/ human energy.*

COCKTAIL ENERGY

These three energies (Sun, Cosmos, and Earth) act individually and form a cocktail of energies, from which the human body gets its energy *via* different sources. The best example of this cocktail of energies is *Food.*

The Cosmic energy along with the Sun energy forms *clouds.* This energy enters the earth *via rain* and mixes with the Earth energy. This grows food and the human body consumes this food to get energy. Basically, the energy which we get from the food, is the *cocktail* in the form of *Universal energy.*

ROUTES THROUGH WHICH THE ENERGY ENTERS HUMAN BODY

1. *Through the Lungs:* Respiration is breathing in and out. The atmospheric air which is a part of cosmic energy contains oxygen. All the body cells need oxygen for their survival and normal functioning. The atmospheric air which we breathe into our lungs, provides this oxygen.

   In the lungs, the oxygen is taken up by the blood, whereas carbondioxide, water vapour and other undesirable gases and waste products are thrown out by the blood into the lungs which are ultimately thrown back into the atmosphere through the air which we breathe out.

   Recently, it has been described that there is something else in the atmospheric air, which gives tremendous amount of energy to the body when it is inhaled. No definite name has been given to this something, which has been called as *Prana* or *Chi* or *Ching* etc.

2. *Via Blood Circulation:* Blood saturated with oxygen is called pure blood. This circulates in the whole body, giving oxygen to different tissues/cells and taking waste products and carbon-dioxide from them. This is

how every cell of the body gets its nourishment/
energy for its normal functioning.

3. *Through Skin:* Skin is also an organ of respiration but
   can also absorb energy from the Sun or any other
   source if rubbed into it. As described earlier, there
   are minor as well as mini chakras all over the body in
   the skin, which also absorb the energy from the
   atmosphere.

4. *Through Food:* Different foods produce different
   energies. When ingested the part of food is converted
   into energy and part of it is thrown out as waste
   product. Energy becomes readily available from
   carbohydrates particularly sugars. Proteins provide
   superior form of energy, which is utilized by various
   tissues of the body. Fats provide inferior form of
   energy.

5. *Through Sense-Organs:* Energy can either be absorbed
   into the human body or let out through various sense-
   organs.

   O Eyes can absorb as well as give out energy called
      'visual energy'. Eyes play a very important role in
      showing happiness, emotions, grief and love.

   O Ears mainly absorb energy from the outside in the
      form of sound, which may be spoken sound, sound
      of various instruments or natural sounds like
      lightning and thunder.

   O Tongue mainly works for giving out energy in the
      form of spoken words.

   O Nose is helpful in absorbing energy from the
      nature, like fragrances of flowers and plants, also
      from artificial fragrances like perfumes, oils etc.

   O Sexual organs give out as well as receive vital
      energy, where two energies *i.e.*, male as well as
      female energy unite and become one.

Basically, this is how the human body derives its energy as well as discharges it.

We shall briefly discuss the role of yogic exercises as well as pranayam in relation to energy.

ROLE OF YOGIC ASANAS

When we perform yogic asanas, a group of muscles contracts and the opposite group relaxes. When the muscles relax after contraction the blood rushes to the muscles providing more oxygen, hence more energy reaches those muscles/parts. That is why it is important to relax the body after each asana, so that it gets re-energized.

Moreover, during asanas the endocrine glands also come into action and throw their secretions into the blood stream, hence providing more chemical energy to different parts of the body. It is said that if yogic asanas are performed with stable mind and in a proper way, with positive thinking, they give tremendous amount of energy to the body and make a person feel absolutely fresh and light.

ROLE OF PRANAYAM

Pranayam means regulation of breath. The individual is advised to take, prolonged and deep breaths in a rhythmical manner. The idea is to fill whole lungs with the air, so that more oxygen is drawn in. Rhythm gives enough time to the inhaled air to have gaseous exchange with the blood in the lungs.

Different techniques of pranayam help in taking more oxygen to the lungs, give more time for the exchange of gases between inhaled air and blood and throwing out more waste products in the exhaled air, because of forced and prolonged exhalation. This extra oxygen in the blood imparts more energy to the tissues/cells when the blood reaches there. Hence, pranayam is the easiest and best technique by which we can provide more energy to the body. The excessive inhaled air also contains more *prana* or *chi*, which revitalizes the body.

Pure Energy vs Impure Energy

Energy is required for every action we perform. Every organ, every tissue and every cell requires energy to perform its function properly. Whether we take that energy from the breath we inhale, from the food we take, or through the skin from the atmosphere or cosmos, it is immaterial.

If we inhale *pure air* that contains oxygen in higher concentration the quality of energy provided to the body is far superior than if we inhale the *polluted air*. Not only the concentration of oxygen is less in the polluted air, but also it may contain other diffusible poisonous gases which can harm various tissues/systems of the body.

The same principle applies to the food which we eat. Purity of food depends upon its ingredients. In case the food is polluted, the pollutants can cause problems in the absorption of different ingredients of the food, as well as can give rise to various short-term or long-term illnesses because of their toxic effects.

If a person is constantly exposed to polluted atmosphere, his skin will not only develop various types of allergies and diseases, but also it will affect the mental and psychological development of the individual. This is the reason that our ancestors preferred to settle along the banks of rivers or streams because the atmosphere around that area is most natural and almost absolutely pure.

19

External Energies which Influence Vital Energy

The following external energies increase or potentiate the effect of vital energy.

1. *Vibrational Energy:* Vibrations, produced by musical instruments, clapping and laughing produce energy. The vibrations produced by the sound and musical instruments are not only pleasing to the ears, but also energizing to various chakras.

○ *Clapping* produces a similar effect. Clapping energizes the human body in different ways. It stimulates the minor chakras present on the palm as well as fingertips. It also energizes the body by the vibrations which are produced while clapping. Clapping also stimulates the acupressure points on the hands.

○ *Laughing* produces energy by stimulation of various chakras directly, as well by the vibrations and resonance produced by this act.

The sound produced by gushing of water, from various streams or waterfalls, gives an energizing effect to the human body through its vibrations creating a pleasing effect to the ears.

2. *Resonance:* Resonance produced by the temple/
   church bells is very energizing because the mind is
   usually concentrating at such religious places. The
   ringing of temple/church bells produces vibration
   sounds followed by a long resonance. Both of them
   have an energizing effect on the human body.

3. *Echo:* This is a sound which is produced when you
   shout in a tomb or a pyramid. The echo that you get
   back is energizing to the human body. It is said that
   pyramids emit energy and *vastu* specialists are very
   keen on building pyramid shape structures. Perhaps
   this was the reason that ancient kings were keen on
   building pyramid-shape structures; the best example is
   pyramids of Egypt.

4. *Splash energy:* Splashing of water produces energy.
   Splash produces energy in different ways:

   (a) It produces vibration sound, which in turn
       produces energy.

   (b) When a diver or a swimmer takes a dive in the
       swimming pool or running water it produces
       a splash. Striking of the body with the water
       produces electro-magnetic waves, which
       energizes the body.

The body also gets energized by chirping of birds, by
hissing and by so many other ways.

20

Vital Airs (Energies) of Yoga

In Yoga, Ten Pranas or Vital Airs (energies) are described which are:

1. *Prana:* Prana means primary air or force (energy). It is supposed to be centered in the brain and moves downwards towards throat and chest. It governs breathing (Inhalation), swallowing, sneezing, belching and spitting. It is that part of cosmic energy which influences most of the other energies in the body. This energy connects the body with the inner self.

2. *Apana:* This is the downward moving air (energy) centered in the colon (large intestines) and having its seat in the anus. This energy governs all downward impulses and helps in elimination of waste products from the body by the process of urination, defecation, menstruation and outlet for sexual energy. This descending energy brings about devolution/ limitation of consciousness.

3. *Samana:* This is the equalising air (energy), which is centered in small intestines in the area of the navel (belly button) and is the force behind the digestive process *i.e.*, digestion of food.

4. *Udana:* This is upward moving air or energy and is located in the chest and throat. This governs

breathing (exhalation) and speech. It also imparts strength, will power and sharpens memory. It is the determining force of aspirations of our lives.

At death it rises up and connects us with the subtle worlds according to our will and karmas (actions).

Udana, if fully developed, gives us the power to transcend the outer world and imparts various psychic powers and brings about evolution/liberation of the consciousness. Yoga stresses primarily on development of *Udana* energy.

5. *Vyana:* This is pervasive air centered in the heart and is distributed throughout the body *via* the circulation of the blood. This mainly derives its energy from food and breath. It controls the movements of the joints and muscles, discharge of impulse and secretions and provides vigor and vitality.

6. *Naga:* This is the energy, which is required for *belching,* meaning bringing the wind up through the mouth.

7. *Kurma:* This is the energy, which controls the movements of eyelids to prevent foreign matters entering the eyes, it also prevents very bright light entering the eyes, hence helps us in opening our eyes and visualizing the things clearly.

8. *Krkla:* This prevents substances passing up the nasal passages, and down the throat, by making one sneeze or cough. This energy also excites our *hunger* and acts as an *appetizer.*

9. *Devaditta:* This is the energy that provides for the intake of extra oxygen in a tired body by enabling us to *yawn.*

10. *Dhananjaya:* This is the energy or the air, which *nourishes* the body on the whole. This remains in the body even after death and some times makes the *corpse to blow up.*

21

Yantra Energy

WHAT ARE YANTRAS?

Yantras are visual devices symbolizing energy pattern of a particular deity. Yantra consists of a visual figure which conforms to the body or form of a deity, whereas energy is provided by *Mantra* which acts as mind, spirit or consciousness. As body is dear to the mind/spirit, so a yantra is dear to the deity.

When a yantra is adopted for worship, the energy is invoked in it, so it becomes a deity himself. Every yantra is a dwelling place of a deity by whose name it is known.

In Sanskrit, 'yantra' means something which gives you liberation from death. Here, liberation means Moksha and death means a cycle of birth and rebirth. This makes yantra a reflection of the divine.

Yantra is used as a tool to withdraw consciousness from the outer world and direct it to the inner world. Hence, this is a concentrated field of consciousness that pulls together and controls different types of energies.

Yantra is a complete geometrical design or a mystical diagram in which a Mantra (usually in Sanskrit) is incorporated. Usually, yantras are engraved on copper, gold, silver and other metallic sheets.

Shape of Yantras

These are generally composed of:

1. A dot or a bindu
2. Circle
3. Triangle
4. Square
5. Star
6. Lotuses
7. Any other form

1. *Dot or Bindu:* A dot is a small circle, the center of which is represented by a point from where the kinetic energy radiates outwards reaching the circumference, before subsiding into the nucleus or the   center.
   It represents the seat of the universe, which is unitary state of *Shiva and Shakti.* From a spiritual point of view, it is *sahasrara,* the thousand-petalled lotus at the Crown Chakra, which is the seat of supreme consciousness.
2. *Circle:* This represents the rhythmic constriction and expansion of cosmic energy in cyclic form.
3. *Triangle:* This is symbolic of creative energy. The triangle with its apex pointing downwards represents the *Shakti* aspect of creation and apex pointing upwards is the *Shiva* aspect.
      As bindu is the center of consciousness, triangle is a place of creativity, which stands for the first stage in the outward movement from pure, unalloyed consciousness.
4. *Square:* The four corners of the square represent four directions, meaning totality of space. Because the entire universe is located in this space, the square often appears as the base of the *yantra.*
5. *Star:* This is a combination of an upward pointing

and a downward pointing triangle representing male and female energies. This superimposition of two symmetrical patterns brings about a balance of two energies.

6. *Lotus:* The lotus represents yantras connected to the seven major chakras in the body. Mythologically, *Brahma,* the creator was born from the lotus. In the yantra, it represents the power that unfolds the universe. It also stands for a healthy and balanced living, because the lotus grows in the mud, yet blossoms above the water. This is symbolic of *how to live in the world while remaining unaffected by it.*

7. *Any other form:* These can be represented by visual and auditory forms of eternal vibrations of divine energy contained in the Yantra.

The exact placement of these mantras helps the seeker to locate those precise vibrations of divine energy in his own body. According to yogis there is perfect correspondence between a yantra and human body.

In tantric literature, it is described that energy contained in yantras is representative of Gods and Goddesses. Without yantra, worship of a particular deity is fruitless. Different yantras are related to different deities, hence are combined with the mantras related to that particular deity. Yantras don't have energy themselves, but it is the mantras which make them vibrate.

Process of Making a Yantra

Depending upon the deity, whom we want to invoke, an auspicious time of a particular day and month is chosen, so as to harness the positive forces. The yantra is first purified. A specially trained person performs a special ritual for this purpose. The mantra is breathed into the yantra innumerable times to make it live and effective.

History of Yantra

The history dates back to 500–1000 BC during the period of Mahabharata.

Sage Durvasa stayed with Sura (grandfather of Lord Sri Krishna) for a year. Kunti, Sura's daughter, served the sage and took care of him. Pleased with Kunti's care, Durvasa gave her the divine mantra of *Sun God*. The sage explained to Kunti that, if she chanted this mantra with pure intentions then she would please the *Sun God,* who in turn will bless her with a son who will be very powerful.

Kunti had a doubtful mind and decided to test the efficacy of the mantra. She started reciting the mantra whole-heartedly and with pure intentions. The *Sun God* appeared and granted her the promised son. Kunti conceived immediately and gave birth to Karna without going through nine-month gestation period.

Karna was born with a metal armour (yantra) on his body, and this grew with him as he grew, and created a powerful protective shield around his body, that made it impossible for the *Pandavas* to kill him in war.

Pandavas went to *Indra* the chief of gods, and asked for his help in killing *Karna*. It was *Indra* who coaxed Karna to remove the yantra, hence Arjuna was able to kill him.

Since then the power of *yantra* is said to provide protection against all negative forces.

Uses of a Yantra

Yantras are used as an aid for prosperity or for the fulfilment of a wish. Yantras can help us conceive, make us monetarily prosperous, enhance our performance at work, and even fulfil our other wishes. Yantras can be tailor-made to control your temper. You can wear them on your body or hang them in your room. They are particularly useful for those who are unable to chant Sanskrit mantras.

A wrong kind of yantra, made in a wrong way, can be harmful. Yantras can also be used for meditation *i.e.*, they can be meditated upon. Some people keep yantras on altars, believing that they will emit spiritual vibrations, whereas others use them as decoration pieces.

Yantras emerging from the body are called *self-born yantras.* A fully realized master like *Sai baba* gives his students or devotees such self-born yantras.

Varieties of Yantras

1. *Shakta yantras:* These yantras represent the divine mother in various forms. Ten forms of divine mother (shakti) have been described, which are *Kali* (Maha-kali), *Tara, Shodashi* (Tripur Sundari), *Bhuvaneshwari* (Rajrajeshwari), *Chinna-masta* (Chinna), *Bhairvi* (Tripur Bhairvi), *Dhumavati* (Alakshmi), *Bagla Mukhi, Matangi* and *Kamla* (Lakshmi). Besides these, there are *Durga* yantra, *Saraswati* yantra and *Gayatri* yantra.

2. *Vaishnava yantras:* These are related to Vishnu and include Ram yantra, *Vishnu* yantra, *Shri Gopal* yantra and *Hanuman* yantra.

3. *Shiva yantras:* These are related to Shiva and include *Bhairav* yantra, *Maha Mrityunjaya* yantra and *Mritsanjivni* yantra.

4. *Architectural yantras:* These are used for planning places of worships like temples and include *Mandala* yantras and *Chatra* yantras. These yantras are usually engraved on the ceiling above the seat of the goddess.

5. *Astrological yantras:* These yantras are used for working with the energy of nine planets (Sun, Moon, Mars, Mercury, Jupiter, Venus, Saturn, Rahu and Ketu).

6. *Numerical yantras:* These are composed of basic geometrical forms but contain numbers and sound as mantras. Some of these are created as magic squares and are used as *talismans.*

I would like to mention here some special forms of yantra, which are:

1. *Sri Yantra:* This is supposed to be the king of yantras and makes one prosperous and has the power to protect one from the god of death. Legend has it, that this yantra originated in the house of a Kashmiri pandit, who was blessed by Lord Shiva with Sri Yantra, which has the energies of the entire universe represented in it. The central area of this yantra is occupied by interlocking triangles representing the *goddess Laxmi.* This yantra can be made in gold, silver, or copper depending upon the position of Sun in one's *horoscope.* The ritual pooja for one full week should be started on Monday only, because this is the day of Lord Shiva.

2. *Hebrew Yantras:* Hebrews combined the numbers with words. For example, *1* represents *A*, a row of these numbers vertically as well as horizontally are written, making sure that the total horizontally as well as vertically comes to 66. This is then put in a *talisman* or *taabiz* and that is energized by chanting mantras to make it effective.

Conclusion: To invoke divine shakti along the lines of a yantra is elaborate and long ritual, described in scriptures as *pran pratishtha.* However, for a seeker who has been initiated by a proper master, these yantras are of little or of no value, because such a student/person knows that most complete yantra is the *human body itself.*

22

Sex Energy

From time immemorial sex energy is thought to be most powerful energy. Perhaps it brings another life into existence by breathing energy into it.

Sexuality and spirituality have long had a conflicting relationship. Some people even see them as rivals that one should be persued and other denied. To become spiritual we need to overcome desire, renounce sexuality and rise above our feelings. Sex energy is produced by the desire. In Geeta, the Lord Krishna has emphasized, 'I am the greatest desire, that is sexual desire'.

So much importance has been given to sexual acts and enjoyment it can bring to the souls of the couples that special shastras have been written on this subject in different cultures/ countries.

Highest form of enjoyment is ananda and this ends up in liberation of soul. Sex energy is thought to be the purest and toughest form of energy; the exchange of which can lead to ananda. Sex is supposed to be the greatest desire in the human beings.

Importance of sex energy was realized in ancient times, when manuals were written on this subject. Kamasutra was written in India over two thousand years ago. *Perfumed*

Gardens was written in Arabia. *Tao of Sex* was written in Japan and *Pillow Books* were written in China.

Ancient Hindu scriptures describe four paths for enlightenment:

1. *Dharma, i.e.,* corrects moral and social behavior.
2. *Artha, i.e.,* material, wealth and comforts.
3. *Kama, i.e.,* love, physical and sexual pleasures.
4. *Kaivalya, i.e.,* enlightenment.

Common Hindus picked up artha and kama for liberation. Ancient religions of India, Arabia, China and Japan saw comforts in food, drink and sex as being not only essential but also unsurpassable urges. Obviously, if these urges cannot be suppressed then they should be put to the best use and perfection, to attain a higher spiritual life.

Sexual desires are deeply embedded in the human psyche and any cleansing process by way of meditation can manifest in the form of *erotic dreams.* Sexuality infused with energy brings divine into act of pleasure drawing us upwards and outwards.

Our ancestors thought that semen is vital fluid, so full of energy, that it can beat *kundalini energy.* It was said that vital fluid should not be wasted. If it is preserved in the body, it can give immense amount of energy, hence *abstinence* was advised and *brahmacharya* was promoted. It was thought that part of human energy is expressed as *sex energy* which when checked and controlled gets changed into *oja* (Spiritual Energy).

Oja is stored in brain and such a man becomes very powerful, he becomes more intellectual, more spiritual and impressive in his speech. *Oja* increases the memory tremendously. Contrary to that, indulgence in sex was advised for married people for the sake of *procreation* only, and not as a form of enjoyment.

It is also described that people can attain highest meditative state through the act of sexual intercourse.

Modern sexologists laugh at the traditional Indian idea of conserving *vital energy*, saying that if the vital fluid is not let out, it will find its way out in the form of wet dreams, like any other secretion of the body. Semen is secretion of endocrine gland (testes), it keeps on forming and accumulating in the passages till it is released out. Too much of indulgence in sex can lead to sex related problems and sexually transmitted diseases.

In the recent times, *Osho* was the person who promoted sex and preached that relaxation of tension through sexual desires/acts can lead to *enlightenment and liberation of soul.*

Tantrik philosophy believes that man is required to move through four stages sexually. These are:

1. Auto sexuality between the age of 0–7.
2. Homosexuality between the age of 7–14.
3. Heterosexuality between the age of 14–42.
4. Abstinence after the age of 42.

According to this philosophy, the man's obsession for sex will leave him by the age of 42. He may still perform the sexual act but with the detachment and at this stage spiritual attainment will also reach its climax.

The interpretation of modern sex therapists on these four stages is given in the way that 'most modern men are still stuck in the auto sexual stage'. They do not consider it for their partner's pleasure, and use them as tools for their own gratification. The old saying *'the dirty old man'* is a manifestation of a person who has crossed the age of 42, without leaving behind his sexual desires.

Making love can become a manifestation of giving a selfless act, which can become a form of prayer itself. Through the body, the hearts are touched, the emotions opened, desires expressed, fears realized, security given, and then *souls can be merged.*

Attaining the highest stage of meditation through the act of sharing, God is remembered. So act of making love goes from physical to emotional level and from emotional level to spiritual level where it becomes a prayer to divine. All the human beings come into existence through an act of sexual union, so we cannot deny the truth of our sexual nature. Moreover, sex is only the *first step* in man's spiritual journey and not the last.

Tantrik Buddhists believe that energy can take one of many different forms. It may take orgasmic, meditative, spiritually enlightening or all the three forms. But transformed energy will do what you need at that particular time and moment. It may not be what you want, but it will be what you need, so go with the energy and do not fight with it and you will get everything you need.

Most people think tantra is about sex. This is how it was promoted by Rajnish (Osho), a twentieth century Hindu guru who spent a lot of time in U.S.A. preaching Americans, how to attain liberation through tantra.

Tantra means 'loom', 'technique', 'path', 'way to achieve'. Tantra is a spiritual practice of bringing together opposite energies specifically *Shakti* and *Shiva* (upwards and downwards energies). Sexual union is a sacred act that represents this union at physical plane. These energies are ultimately balanced at *heart chakra*.

Tantra seeks enlightenment, not by renouncing but by embracing the full experience. A tantric finds ultimate pleasure in senses, desires and feelings, and focuses the expansion of consciousness that comes from sensate connections, to life. Tantra is a harmonious weaving of opposites like mortal and divine, male and female, Shiva and Shakti, spirit and matter, heaven and earth. Through the bonding power of love all things eventually find their way to connection and wholeness. Only love can lift us out of violence and aggression and can bring wholeness that has been severed from each other, we as integrated individuals can open our hearts to create a connection between heaven and earth.

Sexual energy has always been given importance in every ancient religious culture. In Hindu culture, 'Shivaits' meditate upon Shiva-Linga, which represents Shiva's phallus. Buddhists think of sexual organism as 'union with god'. In tantrik sexuality, best of the techniques have been drawn from ancient books of different cultures and different periods of history, which not only tell you how to improve your love-making, but also teach you to change your sexual focus from one of mere pleasure/procreation, to attainment of higher spiritual nature.

In East, sex is a journey with no destination. An *orgasm* may be a stop (station) along the way but it is not end of line, whereas in West, sex stops at *orgasm*. Hindu texts believe orgasm as a spiritual experience and it should be enjoyed as a religious practice.

'Taoists' believe that male orgasm, known as *peak of ching-ching* here applies to spirit, could be separated from ejaculation. Ching, spirit can be both physical (sperm) and etheral (energy). Men, who ejaculate at orgasm, are losing both physical and spiritual ching. They recommend that man should try to hold physical part of ching, as much as possible because losing ching can cause ill health and retaining ching promotes long life and good health.

Orgasm and *ejaculation* are two separate processes, orgasm is a mental process, whereas ejaculation is a physical process and these can be separated.

Tantra says whenever you are in a sexual act, you should shed your guilt and fears, do not repress or resist. Forget yourself, throw all your inhabitations, and feel the music of the harmony of the two energies, then you will forget 'who you are.' There is no 'I' and two energies will become one. There will be no thinking, no future, only *present* and you are in meditation *i.e.*, one with *universe*. Here the sexual act ceases to be an act, it becomes a fragrance and after a while this fragrance is also gone, and only *smadhi* remains. Here you are librated because you have transformed the love into meditation and meditation into love, so *meditation and love become one*. All energies are friendly, only one has to know how to use them. So use the normal sex energy for meditation. In deep penetration, god, meditation and love become one.

Gunas also play an important role in sexual union. If male and female union takes place under relaxed circumstances and both the parties involved have sattvic characters, it gives rise to an offspring who is very intelligent, *sattvic* in character, very compassionate, just like a Rishi. If both the parties are *rajsik* in nature, the offspring is likely to be a warrior, protector of the community and religion and wealth earner. If both the parties are *tamsik* (or if it is a case of rape), then the offspring is likely to be of *tamsik* nature and may end up as a criminal.

I would like to conclude by giving one more view of the strongest form of energy called *kundalini energy*. It is said that *kundalini*, which is a form of sex energy, when calm lies curled up in the feet of her beloved in the Muladhara (first) Chakra. When provoked it starts rising up, making a person agitated and only gets calmed when it reaches the Ajna (sixth) Chakra where it unites with its lover *Shiva*. After getting pacified it travels downwards and goes back to cling to the feet of her lover. Union of a *He* and *She* is just like a union of *Shiva* and *Shakti* which gives a real bliss.

23

Spiritual Intelligence

I am adding this small chapter for those readers who are already on the spiritual path, so that they can get the benefit of the latest research.

Being intelligent doesn't mean having a high IQ *i.e.*, Intelligence Quotient.

I have met lots of people who are very intelligent, but have been utter failure in life.

If IQ is combined with EQ *i.e.*, Emotional Quotient this will add to level of true intelligence.

Intelligence combined with emotional stability works wonders in influencing other people. To be really smart, besides having a high IQ & high EQ you need to have a high SQ *i.e.*, Spiritual Quotient.

Spiritual Quotient is necessary foundation for effective functioning of Intelligence Quotient as well as Emotional Quotient. Intelligence Quotient plus Emotional Quotient plus Spiritual Quotient is equal to ultimate intelligence.

There are so many clever people who feel dejected from life, and feel a sort of emptiness in their lives. They are seeking 'meaning' in their working lives.

To spend life, you need to work. You should do that work, which gives you enjoyment and satisfaction. The other side of the coin is that you need to earn money to satisfy your desires. You may earn as much money as you like to be spent on yourself, but you will never feel satisfied.

The feeling that you get by doing something, for somebody else (may be one of your family members) is very satisfying, and this satisfaction gives a person happiness.

People with spiritual intelligence have the ability to assess that one course of action is more meaningful than the alternative course, and they plan their future to solve problems in a different way, which adds different values to their lives.

How can one acquire Spiritual Quotient (SQ)? It is a big question?

It entails developing some principles or a set of principles in which one believes in, which can be applied to all areas of one's life. You must be aware of your principles all the time and apply them when the time and need arises.

Different personality types will have different principles, some people enjoy creating, others enjoy achievements, some are investigative, others are professionals, some are enterprising, others enjoy leadership some enjoy loyalty others are conventional etc.

Lots of times your principles will evolve around a problem and finding the best solution for it.

The ultimate answer to all these questions is that we are all born to do a particular work, and that work should be such which we should enjoy. Helping others is always a matter for enjoyment, and brings a rare kind of peace of mind.

24

Meditation

We are products of elements, gunas and Brahma (soul, the supreme). If the soul is separated, we become products of our gunas (past karmas), elements and Prakriti (Maya). Prakriti is Nature, every thing has its own prakriti. Prakriti is also synonymous with female energy and Maya. Maya is illusionary, which means it is not everlasting. Maya brings in fear, envy, hate, grief, anger and desires. As described elsewhere in this book, the soul is ensheathed with Maya, but these sheaths can be shed off by the greater knowledge of the soul, but the sheath of Maya i.e., illusion does not allow us to see the soul. Soul can only be seen by mental renunciation. Maya is cause of all sufferings like tension, anxiety, frustration etc. The sheath of Maya can be shed by meditation, which makes us realize the supreme (cosmic energy), of which soul is a tiny fraction.

We shall now proceed to define the process of meditation, types of meditation, stages of meditation and effects of meditation.

WHAT IS MEDITATION?

Meditation is a power, which resists our slavery to Maya. Meditation helps to calm down agitated and turbulent mind and prevents it from running after the senses.

Meditation is a technique for calming, energizing and clarifying the mind.

Purpose of Meditation

The purpose of meditation is to train the mind to enter the higher stage of consciousness and to evade the petty concerns/incidences, which usually occupy the mind.

What does meditation do?

1. It creates contentment.
2. It allows a person to live in the present.
3. It channelizes ego.
4. It opens up the closed energy chakras.
5. It makes the Kundalini shakti to rise.
6. It makes us realize the super conscious state.
7. It enables us to attain bhakti.
8. It enables us to attain mukti (liberation).

Most of the people who go to temple/church/mosque to concentrate and recite God's name, they are all at pre-meditative stage and they remain at this stage throughout their lives, unless they wish and work to reach the advanced stages of meditation, for which they have to be patient, persuasive and regular. A stage of joy is attained in due course of time, where no misery can hurt you.

Yoga teaches one how to attain the supreme stage. Or how to attain Brahma. Religion cannot teach one this, because religion gets stuck at premeditative stage.

Mind is the product of thoughts and is always restless, difficult to control. Mind is an instrument for thinking and has intricate functions. The meditation controls the mind.

Maharishi Patanjali has described five states of mind, which are:

1. *Kshipta state:* In this state, mind hankers after objects. Mental forces are scattered and disarrayed, and are in a state of neglect.

2. *Vikshipta state:* In this state, mind remains agitated and distracted. There is a strong tendency to enjoy the fruits of one's efforts, and the desires are uncontrolled.

3. *Mudha state:* In this state, mind is stupid, foolish and dull. It can not decide what it wants.

4. *Ekagra state:* In this state, mind is alert and attentive, mental faculties are concentrated on a single object. It is one-pointed concentration. Ekagra mind has superior intellectual powers and knows exactly what it wants, uses these powers to achieve its goals.

5. *Niruddha state:* In this state, mind, intelligence and ego are all restrained. All these faculties are involved in serving the almighty (God). There is no feeling of *I* or *mine.* The mind, intellect and ego of such a person merge with the Lord and become one with him.

It is uncontrollable human mind that gets stuck by its own desires, and gets stung by the scorpion of jealousy, grief, anger, pride, hatred etc.

Prerequisites for Meditation for a Beginner

1. Meditation should be done at a segregated special place, which should be cleaned properly, after cleaning it becomes a sacred place.

2. Enter the room with a clean body (after taking bath) and clean mind (after prayer).

3. Keep some fresh flowers in the room so that you get some sweet fragrance. Same environ can be attained, by burning incense. Enter the room with a calm mind. No anger, no unholy thoughts (this will make the room holy). Fragrance gives extra energy to the body.

4. Asana for meditation: Here asana means the seat on which one sits for the meditation. Lots of different things have been recommended for this purpose.

Some of which are as simple as a mat, a cushion or kausa grass. Tiger skin, woollen carpet, silk carpet, a dari (carpet), etc. have also been recommended. Some people are very keen to be comfortable, whereas others are keen to activate the pressure points. Selection of an asana should depend upon the time one wants to spend on meditation. If the meditation is for a short period then it is better to sit on a comparatively rough material, because it activates the pressure points whereas if the meditation is to be done for a long period, then the comfort must be kept in mind.

5. Never practise meditation when you are ill, lazy or miserable.

6. Before starting the meditation pay homage to your guru and parents.

7. Meditate preferably on an empty stomach because blood circulation is uniform throughout the body when the stomach is empty. You may meditate once a day or twice a day depending upon your daily routine.

8. Always start the meditation with the prayer for the welfare of the whole world.

9. Sit for some time and analyze the thoughts in your mind. Gradually, you will observe that these thoughts get less and less.

10. Get rid of distractions.

11. Be kind and respectful to yourself. Do not criticize yourself and love yourself.

12. Gradually practise meditation hard, not working for the result. Bring the mind to a single direction.

    The mind is darkness in tamsik people, it is power in rajsik people whereas it is calm and serene in sattvik people.

13. Gradually you will be able to control all negative energies like anger, pride, hatred etc.

14. Last but not the least you should have a complete belief in what you are doing.
15. Always open your heart completely in meditation.

Stages of Meditation

Osho recommends four-stage meditation for a beginner.

1. *Ordinary thinking:* In this stage, one should allow al' sorts of thoughts to come into mind. This is called multi-directional thinking. With practice the mind starts settling down.
2. *Contemplation:* In this stage, the mind gets trained for thinking in a particular direction. This is called unidirectional thinking.
3. *Concentration:* In this stage, the mind is focused at a single point or bindu. There is no movement of thought/mind at all.
4. *Meditation:* In this stage, there is no thinking because there is no mind. The mind is blank.

"Love is the best method of meditation." It (love) should be selfless and not a lust, with no intention of possessiveness. When energy has to be released, why release it through anger or tension or frustration, why not release it through love.

In Yoga, meditation has been described in three stages:

1. *Concentration:* Here you put your mind only on one object, which may be your own breath, tip of your nose or any other object. Keep your mind steady on that particular object and you will learn to concentrate sooner or later depending upon your past and present karma.
2. *Dhyana:* In this stage, which is the next stage after concentration, you loose the identity with your physical body and environment. This can only be attained after regular and continuous practice.

3. *Samadhi:* In this stage, the mind is totally absorbed in God/Brahma. All the energy channels, which control the senses of the body and universe, are forced into the mind, so that the mind is turned upon the universe itself. Once you come out of Samadhi, which is the most wonderful experience, you feel you had most beautiful rest of your life. Power of meditation gives you everything.

Realization of God/universe is bhakti, total freedom from all bondage is mukti. Once you realize the God by turning your mind inwards, your mind wants to unite with the God. Once you have trained your mind to concentrate on a single object, the mind can be further trained to concentrate without any object and this is the stage of super consciousness or *Samadhi.*

In Rajayoga, which is the practical way to attain super consciousness, Maharishi Patanjali has devised eight ways to reach that state, which are:

1. *Yama:* This is the initial stage in which one is advised to govern his life with five principles: (a) Do not injure any other person by thoughts, words or deed; (b) Have non-covetousness in thoughts, words or deed; (c) There should be perfect justice in thoughts, words or deed; (d) There should be perfect truthfulness in thoughts, words or deed; and (e) Non-receiving of gifts from any source.
2. *Niyama* is regularity for the care of the body and personal hygiene like exercising, taking daily bath etc.
3. *Asana* means yoga postures to relax the body.
4. *Pranayam:* Control of the breath.
5. *Pratyahara:* Turning the mind inwards and restraining from going outwards.
6. *Dharana:* To concentrate on one object.
7. *Dhyana:* Meditation.
8. *Samadhi:* Attainment of super consciousness/Brahma.

Here physical and mental purity along with perseverance are described as the main objects to attain Dhyana. Mind has a great thinking capacity, which if not controlled is wasted, when controlled it becomes a wonderful power. It is wastage of time to find God outside, because "I am Brahma" *i.e.*, God is inside me. Hence, human body is the greatest temple housing the God within it. You have your past, present and future inside you, try to accumulate your power in silence and you will become a dynamite of spirituality.

Meditation brings light to the mind, which can only shine with the help of light of Brahma. There is a state beyond the conscious plane where there is no duality of the knower and knowledge. Normally, we become slave of our body, slave of our mind, slave of the world, slave of passions and slave of death. This slavery can only be broken through Meditation on Brahma.

Nobody is watching your action from outside except the Brahma, within you. Once you realize that, there is God within everybody, you can see brahma in everything *i.e.*, life, death, sorrow, and happiness. There is no birth or death for you. There is no misery or desire for you.

It is normally said that to develop *spirituality* you need help of a *Guru* because soul can easily receive impulses from another soul. Guru is the only person who can *light the lamp of spirituality*. It's not very easy to find a genuine guru these days. But if you can practise the following, you may be able to attain the goal without a guru.

- O Restraining the mind from going outside.
- O Restraining the senses.
- O Turning the mind inwards.
- O Suffering without grumbling.
- O Stick the mind to one particular idea.
- O Think of your real nature.
- O Get rid of all superstitions.
- O Do not have any inferiority complex.

Techniques of Meditation

Numerous techniques of meditation have been described and one can adopt any technique which one finds convenient. Some of the commonly used techniques are described below:

1. Regulating or concentrating on one's own breathe.
2. Gazing at an image like candle flame or a symbol.
3. Recitation of mantras.
4. Following one's own thoughts.
5. Free flowing, non-specific movements of body.
6. Walking silently.
7. Concentrating on a problem.
8. Visualizing movement of energy up and down your own body.
9. Listening to music with attention.
10. Relaxing and analyzing the ideas coming to your brain.
11. Guided visualization or transcendental meditation.

Ways of Meditation

By meditation, we try to connect our mind with the supreme to attain the state of bliss. Different ways are adopted to connect our energy with the mother energy. Some of commonly adopted methods/ways are described here.

Sound Meditation

Energizing part in the sound are the vibrations. Sound may be vocal, instrumental, natural or artificial. When a sound is pleasing to the ears, it gets deeper into your thought, which in turn vibrates the brain cells, which produce certain chemicals leading to production of energy, which take you into a state of ecstasy. To produce this effect, we chant certain mantras (Hindu philosophy), which have a purifying and meditative effect on the mind as well as the body.

A relaxed mind always leads to a relaxed body, through the action of the nerves, but the *vice versa* may not be true. A relaxed body can have a tense mind, which in turn will lead to a tense body.

In Hindu philosophy/mythology, vibrations produced by chanting the word AUM produce a very soothing energy, which has a calming effect on the mind.

AUM is a Sanskrit word meaning *All*, which conveys the concept of omnipresence, omnipotence and omniscience. AUM is thought to be the best praise of the almighty. AUM is composed of three syllables and when written in sanskrit has a crescent and a dot on its top.

Different religious Gurus have interpreted the word AUM, in their own way. Some of those interpretations are:

1. In AUM, A symbolizes the waking state, U the dream state, and M the dreamless state of the mind and spirit. The entire symbol with crescent and dot combines all the states, which is state of samadhi.

2. In AUM, A symbolizes the absence of desire, U absence of fear and M absence of anger. The whole word stands for perfect man, one whose wisdom is firmly established in God.

3. In AUM, A stands for present, U for past and M for future. The entire symbol stands for the creator who transcends the limitations of time.

4. In AUM, each syllable depicts the stages of yogic discipline namely Asana, Pranayam and Pratyahara. The entire symbol stands for Samadhi.

5. Each syllable in AUM stands for three gunas *i.e.*, sattva, rajas, and tamas. The whole word AUM represents one who has gone beyond the pull of all these gunas.

6. Each syllable in AUM symbolizes speech, mind and breath of life (Prana), while the entire word stands for divine spirit.

7. AUM represents the triad of divinity namely Brahma the creator, Vishnu the sustainer, and Shiva the destroyer of the universe.

Other mantras are described under the Japa meditation.

Dhyana Meditation

Dhyana is the Vedic word for meditation, the precursor of which is concentration. It is the one-pointed concentration, penetrating intuition, and refined comprehension, which helps you to detach from ordinary life.

Meditation strengthens your mind, develops the power of concentration, and makes you successful.

Hence, meditation makes you realize the absolute truth, which is the ultimate knowledge, by raising the rays of your consciousness.

Yoga Meditation

Yoga is samadhi, which is meditation without any objective consciousness. Meditation is means to yoga. Yoga relaxes the body and mind and makes them perfect for the thought process. If the thought process is channelized properly, then the whole functioning of body is in a methodical way. Yoga and meditation check the hyper activity of thought process and convert it into tranquility.

Tapas Meditation

Tapas means austerity with intense concentration in a stable meditative posture till the attainment of the higher self (super consciousness).

Japa Meditation

Japa is repeated recitation of mantras according to your ishtdev or God or presiding deity.

Gayatri mantra is thought to be supreme of all the mantras of Vedas. It is a universal mantra, which can be used for universal energy. In Gayatri mantra which is

"Om Bhur Bhuvah Swah That-Savitur Varenyam Bhargo Devasya Dhiemahi Dhiyo Yo Nah Prachodayat."

We meditate on the God's glory, which has created the universe, which is embodiment of knowledge and light, who is remover of all sins and ignorance, He may enlighten our intellect, and we worship Him.

Mantras can also be recited with the string of beads.

Usually there are 108 beads in a string and this signifies the 108 names of devi (Goddess) i.e., female form of God.

You may meditate on any mantra pertaining to the God, deity or religion you believe in.

How to Meditate

1. *Regularity* in time and place is important for meditation. The best time to meditate is between 4 to 6 a.m., because at that time the atmosphere is charged with spiritual forces and body is fully charged with energy.

   It is quiet all around; one feels fresh after sleep and has a clear mind.

   The next best time is the dusk, when the Sun has just set, because again the atmosphere is highly charged by the spiritual energy.

2. *Posture:* It is always best to sit in the erect position, and for that the best is Lotus position in which the spine is always erect.

   The erect posture helps the energy travelling up along the spine.

   Always try to face the east or north to take the advantage of favorable magnetic vibrations.

3. *Breathing:* Regulate your breathing by taking few long and deep Yogic breaths. A regulated rhythm of inhaling and exhaling makes the energy reach every cell of the body. With practice body becomes one with the breath.

4. *Concentration on Ajna Chakra:* Concentrate all your energies at your Ajna Chakra with single-pointed mind and sense the duality disappearing and becoming one with the God/Mother energy.

5. *Stage of Samadhi:* This is the stage of extra sensory perception where your consciousness completely merges with the divine energy and you become one with Jesus, Krishna and Allah.

Experiences during Meditation

Different meditators have enumerated the following experiences:

1. Change in body temperature. Body temperature may go up as well as down during the process of meditation.
2. Light headedness.
3. Tingling around scalp, hands or feet.
4. Involuntary muscular jerks.
5. Flowing of tears.
6. Runny nose.
7. Coughing.
8. Yawning.
9. Perceiving lights of different shapes and colors. Usually different tattwas are represented by different colors *e.g.*, *earth* is yellow, *water* is white, *fire* is red, *air* is green and *space* is blue. Lights may be white or of different colors and different shapes like Moon, Sun, Stars etc. As the consciousness increases the lights get bigger and brighter.
10. Perceiving different shapes or symbols.

In the beginning, it is very difficult to interpret the symbols, but with the experience the mind starts defining the symbols. As a matter of fact one is in a semiconscious state when one starts perceiving lights and symbols. In later stages when one has really attained great practice of meditation one can see lights and symbols while going to bed or while waking up from sleep.

Reported Effects of regular meditation

The following are some of the effects reported by regular meditators:

1. Increased or better physical health.
2. Better clarity of mind.
3. Better concentration.
4. Increased creativity.
5. Greater productivity at work.

6. Increased satisfaction.
7. Increased well-being.

Physiological changes in the body during Meditation

The undermentioned physiological changes have been described while the body is going through a process of meditation:

○ Body oxygen uptake is reduced by 20 to 25 per cent.
○ Heartbeat rate is reduced by up to 25 per cent.
○ Body metabolic rate is reduced.
○ Blood pressure is lowered.

This allows the body to go into a state of complete rest, which alerts the awakened conscious. It also increases awareness, because mind is released from body's limitations and gets free to expand in new horizons.

○ There is a better co-ordination between right and left hemispheres of the brain, leading to better perception.
○ True meditation is a state of mind, which once achieved begins to create its own rhythm, field and vibration around us, till it becomes integral part of our life and gives joy and happiness to life.

Obstacles in Meditation

1. *Cessation of Practice:* After few sessions people cannot concentrate and give up. Try changing the place, timing or posture for bringing the mind to a single point, these things might help.
2. *Diet:* Healthy body and healthy mind are prerequisites for meditation. Body can be kept healthy by performing certain Yoga asanas and regular pranayam can keep mind healthy. For healthy body and healthy mind, sattvik diet, fresh air and adequate rest are essential. Body can be purified and kept in a healthy state by regular *fasting.* As a matter of fact, body is the

physical portion of diet, so always eat fresh and pure food. Do not drink any intoxicating drinks. Do not smoke.

3. *Physical Fitness:* A fit body is always a boon, so regular exercise, reasonable sleep can always help in meditation, whereas lack of exercise, too little or too much of sleep, consumption of drugs, mental worries, excessive sexual activity, wrong food are hindrances to meditation.

    Laziness and drowsiness are the universal obstacles to meditation, so is over indulgence in sleep. Brain needs rest only for a short time. A mind, which is used to meditation does not require a lot of sleep. In meditation, the body is light and mind is cheerful. In sleep body is heavy and mind is dull. Lethargy and depression are obstacles for meditation.

4. *Unfavorable Environment:* Unsuitable place, undesirable company, company of thieves, greedy people, people indulging in idle gossip are bad for meditation. Any thing, which has lasting impact on the mind, can be a hindrance for the meditation. Loose talk, useless and excess talking, oral diarrhea make a person unfit for meditation. Hyper egoism (too much ego) will not allow the mind to rest at one point, hence is hindrance to meditation. Emotions, anger, envoy, jealousy are the greatest enemies of meditation.

5. *Lack of Faith:* Without faith, realization of God is impossible. Spirituality is based upon faith and possessiveness. If you think that a process will benefit you, then you have to put all your faith into it, only then you can achieve/attain it.

6. *Role of Vital Energy:* In olden days, gurus and sannyasis thought that total control over all the senses was essential for meditation. Control over sexual energy was also preached by leading life as a Brahmachari, because it was thought that sex energy and spiritual

energy is one and the same thing and this was called *oja shakti*. Sex energy moves downwards whereas spiritual energy (Oja) moves upwards. Buddha attained nirvana by total control of all hidden senses, which helped him turning his mind inwards. To attain enlightenment you don't have to abandon sex totally (modern view) but do not over indulge in it. Reduce it gradually and use that energy for the constructive purposes.

7. *Mind:* In the early stages of meditation, bad negative thoughts will come to the mind but with perseverance those thoughts will perish. Thoughts of lust are contagious and are obstacle in the process of meditation.

25

Answers to Some Frequently Asked Questions

Ques.1. Who we are? And what is our place in the world?
Ans.   The answer lies in mindfulness, which means,
        'paying attention'.

        It involves analyzing each moment, under-
        standing their meaning without getting attached to
        any one of them. Mindfulness takes our awareness
        into present moment, bringing full experience
        and satisfaction in life. This also brings past and
        future into the present together (present perfect).
        Enemies of mindfulness include impatience,
        fear, presumptions and disassociations. Each of
        these disconnects us from the present and its
        experiences. Conscious living requires sensitivity
        and responsibility. Impatience makes us rush to the
        future, not realizing the richness of the present.

        Fear does not allow us to engage fully in the
        present. Presumption does not allow the present to
        unfold fully. When we operate by habit, we allow
        our mind to disconnect and are no longer engaged
        in the present.

        Mindfulness brings lots of information whereas
        its enemies restrict the information, giving us

misunderstandings, ignorance and false impressions. Mindfulness is a state of observation (witness).

Ques.2. What is higher Self?

Ans. When we cannot see our way clearly through difficult situations, then we tap our higher Self (vision, imagination, consciousness) to show us the way. There are different opinions on what is higher self, *e.g.*,

(a) It is communing with God or divine intelligence.

(b) This is another aspect of Self, which comes into existence when lower chakras fail us in finding a solution to a problem.

Higher Self is a mystery, which cannot be solved, but it does allow us to receive information that can be used as a guide to bring us closer to wholeness.

Ques.3. How to achieve non-attachment?

Ans. It is very difficult to attain, because when you wish to be detached, you become more attached. In my view, it is best to be attached to every thing, but equally, which becomes non-attachment. It is the degree of attachment which is the cause for troubles.

Ques.4. What is belief system?

Ans. Belief means putting your trust in something. When your consciousness expands your belief system grows with it. Limiting beliefs are our greatest enemy *i.e.*, "I cannot do it", "it is impossible", "I do not deserve it" etc. As a matter of fact, anything and everything is possible, only you have to brush and polish your belief system. It eventually leads to deeper experiences and connects us more with the inner truth.

Ques.5. What is religion?

Ans. *Religion* in Latin means 'to reconnect', as is 'yoga'

to connect with the supreme. The drive towards religion comes from each chakra *i.e.*, need for security from chakra one, emotional needs from chakra two, sense of power from chakra three, sense of community from chakra four, creative expression from chakra five and chance to realize the ultimate truth from chakras six and seven.

Religion does give us structure, a practice, awareness, deeper states of experience and understanding and community support. As a belief system, religion obscures our experience and its morality can obscure true spirituality. Community support, meditation, group singing, rituals, yoga, puja and community services are excellent religious values in our lives. Religion with practice is an active experience, which can further the evolution of the soul.

Ancient spiritual seekers thought that crown chakra is seat of Amrit, which builds the body, because it controls brain and pituitary glands on physical plane. Ancient yogis also thought that this chakra is the seat of Brahma. There is supposed to be a hole in this chakra at the level of interior fontanels and it is said that Brahma after creating human body entered as the soul through this hole. It is also a Hindu belief that if one is pure with yoga sadhana, Prana goes out busting this chakra at the time of the death.

Ques.6. Is spirit and soul, one and the same thing?

Ans.   For a long time spirit was thought to be synonymous with soul. But now, it is thought that these are two separate things. 'Soul' is said to be expression of inward realization within the individual, whereas 'Spirit' seeks limitations from outside of the created world and universality. 'Soul' is gatherer of this spirit. Spirit may or may not be individual as it can take many shapes and forms.

'Soul' is enhanced by the presence of the spirit, as if soul is essence of spirit. When spirit gets anchored to the soul, it gives soul a meaning and a purpose. Soul tends towards manifestation, whereas spirit tends towards liberation.

26

Conclusion

There is definitely something beyond this material world, which pervades everything and is uncreated, so far. This is beyond the reach of human knowledge and understanding. Some people call "that something beyond" as reality, because anything beyond our comprehension always seems 'Real'.

How to Approach that Reality?

- By distinguishing ego from true self.
- By becoming detached.
- By forgetting our preferences.
- By understanding the nature of our desires.
- By not working for personal gains.
- By being humble.
- By being devoted.
- By re-directing our attention.
- By surrendering ourselves.

How to Learn the Above Mentioned?

- From a teacher.
- By the grace of God.
- By dying and being reborn with good karmas.
- By seeing the light through meditation.

○ By experiencing freedom.
○ By being fearless.
○ By experiencing union.

He who hates none is friend of all

○ He is merciful to all.
○ He has nothing of his own.
○ He is free from egoism.
○ He is even-minded in pain and pleasure.
○ He is always satisfied, his self is controlled and his mind and intellect become brahma himself, who cannot be disturbed by others.
○ Who doesn't depend on anything?
○ Who is pure and active?
○ Who doesn't care for the result of his work?

Glossary

Agya	:	To order.
Ajna	:	To perceive.
Anahata	:	Unstuck.
Ananda	:	Supreme enjoyment.
Artha	:	Material values.
Asanas	:	Postural exercises of yoga.
Aura	:	Personal energy field.
Bhakti	:	Realization of God.
Bile	:	Excreted by the liver and stored in gall, Bile helps in digestion of fats.
Brahma	:	The supreme creative energy, the soul.
Brahmacharya	:	Abstinence from sex.
Chakras	:	Circular discs, main lotus of energies, Whirlpools of energy.
Clairaudience	:	People with extra sensory perceptions, who can hear voices of spirits and ghosts.
Clairvoyance	:	People with extra sensory perceptions who can visualize the energy body.
Dari	:	A mat made from weaving cotton threads.
Dharma	:	Social custom, natural law, religious and moral values.
Dharana	:	One-pointed concentration.
Dhyana	:	Regular practice of concentration with empty mind, Meditation.
Deity	:	Hindu God.
Ego	:	Self-identity.
Emancipation	:	Liberation from bondage.
Emotions	:	Strong feelings.
Endocrine Glands	:	These are ductless glands, present in the body, which produce secretions, which are directly thrown

		into the blood. These secretions are vital for overall functioning of the body. Example of endocrine glands are: Pituitary, Adrenals, Ovaries, Testes etc.
Ether	:	The upper regions of the atmosphere, medium believed to fill all space and to support the propagation of electromagnetic ways.
Gayatri Mantra	:	Supreme Vedic mantra to describe the glories of the God.
Gunas	:	Modes of energy depicting character of an individual.
Humors	:	Humors are fluids of the body, which perform important functions.
Kama	:	Physical and sexual pleasures.
Kaivalya	:	Enlightenment.
Karmas	:	Actions, deeds.
Manipura	:	A shining gem.
Mantras	:	Sacred words or syllables used as an object of concentration.
Maya	:	Illusion.
Moksha	:	Salvation, getting free from the cycle of life and death.
Mukti	:	Freedom from all bondage.
Muladhara	:	Base, root.
Musk	:	Kasturi which emits sweet fragrance found in deer's belly.
Nadis	:	Streams, nerves.
Navel	:	Belly button.
Niyama	:	Regularity.
Oja	:	Spiritual energy.
Prakriti	:	Nature.
Prana	:	Life giving ingredient in the inhaled air.
Pranayam	:	Different techniques of breath control.
Pratyahara	:	Turning the mind in words.
Puranas	:	Old Hindu scriptures describing the creation of the universe and recounting the birth and deed of Hindu Gods.
Sacrifices	:	Sacred acts performed to invoke or please Gods.
Sallicial	:	Imaginary a huge structure.
Shiva	:	Supreme hindu diety, male energy, super consciousness, Shiva, Shakti, Supreme Hindu Goddess, female energy.
Shruti	:	Knowledge imparted by a teacher to the pupil by words of mouth.

Samadhi	:	It is a state of mind, where all energy channels lead to God, the supreme energy; State of super consciousness.
Smriti	:	Knowledge imparted through written scripts.
Svadhisthan	:	Seat for taste and enjoyment.
Tapas	:	Austerity with concentration.
Tattvas	:	Elements.
Upanishads	:	Highest aspect of religious truth learnt by a student from his guru by sitting besides him, in the form of a conversation (Questions and Answers), mystical and esoteric doctrine of ancient Hindu Philosophy.
Vastu	:	It is a vedic science which deals in the electromagnetic force of the earth and influence of different planets on this force.
Vedas	:	Hindu Scriptures.
Vishuddha	:	Pure.
Yama	:	Principle for leading healthy and honest life.
Yantra	:	Device in which spiritual energy is incorporated.

Bibliography

Abhedananda Swami, *Yoga Psychology*, Ram Krishna Vedanta Math, Kolkata, India.

Andrews Ted, *How to Develop and Use Psychic Touch*, Llewellyn Publications, St. Paul, Minnesota U.S.A.

Aurobindo Sir, *The Super Mental Manifestation*.

Avalon Arthur, *The Serpent Power*, Dover Publications, New York, U.S.A.

Baker Douglas, *The Techniques of Astral Projection*, Baker Publications, Highroad, Essendon, Herts AL9 6HR, U.K.

Bartlett Sarah, *Auras and How to -do Them*, Collins and Brown Ltd., London SW11 4NQ, U.K.

Buess Lynu, *Numerology in the New Age*, Light Technology, P.O. Box 1495, Sedona, U.S.A.

Chandappa Rohan, *The Little Book of Stress*, Ebury Press, London SW1 V2SA.

Charak K.S. (Dr.), *Surya, the Sun God*, Uma Publications, New Delhi, India.

Chinmayananda Swami, *Meditation & Life*, Chinmaya Nanda Mission, Mumbai, India.

Chinmayananda Swami, *Kaivalya Upanishad*, Central Chinmaya Mission Trust, Mumbai, India.

Chinmayananda Swami, *Kath Upanishad*, Central Chinmaya Mission Trust, Mumbai, India.

Choa Kok Sui Master, *Miracles Through Pranic Healing*, Institute of Inner Studies, Makati City 1200, Philippines.

Craze Richard, *Tantric Sexuality*, Hodder and Stoughton, London, NW 13 BH.

Dalrymple William, *The Age of Kali*, Flemingo — A division of Harper Collins, New York and London.

Dr. Peter J. D'Adams, *Eat Right for Your Type*, Century, London, U.K.

Feuerstein George, *The Yoga Tradition*, Motilal Banarsidass, Delhi, India.

Friedman Thomas, *The World is Flat*, Penguin Books, London, U.K.

Frawley David (Dr.), *Ayurvedic Healing*, Motilal Banarsidass, Delhi, India.

Gawain Shakti, *Creative Visualization*, Full Circle, New Delhi, India.

Gawain Shakti, *Meditation*, Full Circle, New Delhi, India.

Gokhle Namita, *The Book of Shiva*, Penguin Books India Pvt. Ltd., New Delhi, India.

Gopalan C., Sashtri B.V. Rama, Balasubramanian S.C. *Nutritive Value of Indian Foods*, Indian Council of Medical Research, Hyderabad, India.

Greogory P. Fields, *Religion Therapeutics*, Motilal Banarasidas, Delhi, India

Grewal Rohina, *The Book of Ganesha*, Penguine Books India Pvt. Ltd., New Delhi, India.

Hillman James, *The Soul's Code*, Bantam Books, London, U.K.

        Janet Balaskas, *Preparing for Birth with Yoga*, Shaftesbury, Dorset, SP7 8BP, U.K.

Judith Anoda, *Eastern Body, Western Mind*, Celestial Arts, Berkeley, CA, U.S.A.

Judith Anoda, *Wheels of Life*, Llewellyn Publications, St. Paul, Minnesota, U.S.A.

Kavi Jankinath, *Bhavani Nama Sahasra Stutih*, Ram Krishna Ashram, Shree Nagar, India.

Krupp P.G. (Dr.), *Drugless Therapy*, Ocean Books Pvt. Ltd., New Delhi, India.

Levin Michael, *Spiritual Intelligence*, Hodden and Stroughton, London, NW1 3BH, U.K.

Low Jennifer & Danino Michel, *The Mind of the Cells*, Institute of De Recherches Evolutives Paris, France.

Macritchie James, *The Chi King Way*, Harper Collins, 1160, Baltery Street, San Franscisco, CA-94111-1213.

Moore Thomas, *The Planets Within*, Lindisfarne Press, Hudson, New York 12534, U.S.A.

Moss Robert, *Dream Gates*, Three Rivers Press, New York, U.S.A.

Muktananda Swami, *Chit Shakti Vilas*, Ram Krishna Math, India.

Naparstek Belleruth, *Your Sixth Sense*, Harper Collins, 1160, Baltery Street, San Franscisco, U.S.A.

Orloff Judith, *Intuitive Healing*, Rider, London, U.K., Osho, *Book of Secrets*. OSHO, *"Book of Secrets"*.

Paramahansa Yogananda, *Autobiography of Yogi*.

Paramananda Swami, *Vedanta in Practice*.

Peat David F, *Synchronicity*, Bantam Books, New York, U.S.A.

Radha Krishnan (Dr.), *Translation of Gita*.

Reiter Russel J., *Melatonine*, Bantam Books, New York, U.S.A.

Roy Bikek Deb & Roy Dipali Deb, *Atharva Veda, Yajur Veda, Rig Veda*, Books for All, Delhi, India.

Sankracharya, *Eight Upanishads,* Advaita Ashram, India.

Sharma G.C., *Brihat Parasara Hora Shashtra,* Sagar, Janpath, New Delhi, India.

Shepard Leslie, *Living With Kundalini,* Shambhla, Boston (U.S.A.), London, U.K.

Siddhapeeth Gurudev, Ganesh Puri, Maharashtra, India.

Tolle Eckhart, *The Power of Now,* Yogi Impressions, Mumbai, India.

Verma Pavan K., *The Book of Krishna,* Penguin Books, New Delhi, India.

Worldwood Valirie Anu, *Fragment Mind.*

Zukav Gary, *The Seat of Soul,* The Random House Group, London SW1 W2SA.

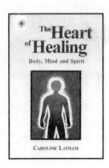

THE HEART OF HEALING: Body, Mind and Spirit —*Caroline Latham*
It is full of practical help and inspiration to stay on the course. It is quiet in-the-mind healing which may involve touching. Is there anyone who would not like to be able to heal himself, his children or loved ones? Don't wait until you are perfect, or think you know enough. All you need is an open heart that allows the healing energies to flow through you.

ISBN: 978-81-7822-019-2

ENERGETIC HEALING: Embracing the Life Force —*Arnie Lade*
Energetic Healing is a guide to the inner landscape of subtle energy. In this ground-breaking book the role, manifestation, utility and healing power of our life force/energy is explored in a concise and informative fashion.

ISBN: 978-81-7822-005-5

QUANTUM-TOUCH: The Power to Heal —*Richard Gordon*
Quantum-Touch represents a major breakthrough in the art of hands-on healing. This book clearly teaches you to use special breathing and body focusing techniques to raise your energy level so high that with a light touch, you can see postural corrections spontaneously occur as bones gently glide back into their correct alignment. Beyond this, pain and inflammation are rapidly reduced and healing is profoundly accelerated.

ISBN: 978-81-7822–009-3

PRANIC LIVING AND HEALING —*Luis S.R. Vas*

Is it possible to live on sunlight and boiled water and no other food? Practitioners of pranic living assure us that it is possible. The practice is called pranic nourishment and its practitioners claim that in the coming decades it may be the answer to global hunger and malnutrition.

ISBN: 978-81-7822-161-8

SPIRITUAL HEALING: Doctors Examine Therapeutic Touch and Other Holistic Treatments —*Dora Kunz*

Healing is a divine art. The book presents a surprising open-mindedness and forward looking vision. In this edition of a classic collection, the best minds in holistic healing explore the spiritual basis of the alternative health care movement.

ISBN: 978-81-7822-011-6

FENG SHUI FOR THE BODY: Balancing Body and Mind for a Healthier Life —*Daniel Santos*

This breakthrough book applies the principles of Feng Shui, the ancient Chinese art of energy flow, to the most intimate house we inhabit—the human body. Daniel Santos shows us how to use the Four Motions—body movement, breath, eye movement, and sound—to maximize the flow of healthful life energy.

ISBN: 978-81-7822-012-3

MAGNETIC HEALING: Advanced Techniques for the Application of Magnetic Forces —*Buryl Payne*

Through this book discover the positive benefits of magnetism for improving your health and well-being. This book will answer all your questions related to magnetic healing.

ISBN: 978-81-7822-002-4

ARCHETYPAL CHAKRAS: Meditations and Exercises for Opening Your Chakras — *Arnold Bittlinger*

The Chakras are the body's own innate memory aids for the path of individuation. This is very significant. Our body constantly reminds us of the developmental processes within our soul.

ISBN: 978-81-7822-084-0

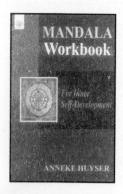

MANDALA WORKBOOK: For Inner Self-Development —*Anneke Huyser*

In this fun and unique book, Anneke Huyser shares the mandala-making methods she has developed over the course of a decade. She gives you just the right amount of background information to inspire you to make your own mandala—a symbol of your journey towards wholeness.

ISBN: 978-81-7822-287-5